PRAISE FOR

Improvising in Italian

"Jennifer's ability to vividly describe her impressions in *Improvising in Italian* takes the reader on a fantastic trip where we, too, get to experience the food, the land, the people—and it's all so delicious! A perfect read for the globally curious—the adventurer at heart!"

—**JESSICA BUCHANAN**, *New York Times* bestselling author of *Impossible Odds*

"Blend together unstoppable love, delectable food, and a craving for adventure. Add fistfuls of mishaps, some funny and others truly scary. Mix with heaping amounts of resilience, and you have a recipe for a sumptuous—and profound—memoir. *Improvising in Italian* is a winning chronicle of the quest for a fully authentic life."

—**DAWN RAFFEL**, author of *Boundless as the Sky*

"Part memoir, part travelogue, Jennifer Artley's *Improvising in Italian* is an honest, compelling, fascinating insider's view of a husband and wife starting a new life together as they take up residence in a small Italian city. Amongst the old-world beauty, culinary delights, and bureaucratic nonsense, they attempt to create a perfect life, just as a mysterious virus, COVID-19, begins to turn the world upside down and inside out. As her husband's various business ideas fizzle and fall apart, Jennifer tries desperately to hold things together, doing her best to support her husband's hopes and dreams, while grappling to make sense of her own life. A gem of a book that'll have you eagerly turning pages to find out what ultimately survives a world in chaos."

—**CHARLES SALZBERG**, award-winning writer, three-time Shamus Award nominee, and author of *Man on the Run*

"Artley's breezy style of writing echoes the improvisational spirit that defines her memoir. When Jennifer Artley and her family move to Modena, Italy, in search of a fresh start, they find themselves swept into the complexities of a new culture and the challenges of familial adjustment, all the while cooking and hosting elaborate Italian meals. Her conversational tone draws readers into her world, making even the most personal struggles relatable and engaging. With courage and vulnerability, she opens herself to curiosity and adventure. Perfect book for fans who's ever dreamed of starting over in a foreign land."

—**DAHLIA ABRAHAM-KLEIN**, author of *Caravan of Hope: A Bukharan Woman's Journey to Freedom*

"In *Improvising in Italian,* Jennifer Artley takes a different approach from the well-trodden romantic notion of starting over in an exotic foreign country.... Artley, who has traveled the world and lived in numerous exotic locations, finds herself and her partner mired in a minefield of awkward business ventures while navigating the morality of being a wealthier immigrant in a country that opened its doors to others who are fleeing for their lives.

"In this painfully honest memoir and perhaps cautionary tale, Artley doesn't mince words about the unsavory side of doing business, the unusual mixture of friendships that develop, and the sheer terror of being in lockdown in Italy during COVID-19. This health scare closed down their business ventures and brought their relationship to a crucial turning point. Her story is philosophical and poignant and offers rare insight into the reality of leading an adventuresome lifestyle."

—**DONNA KEEL ARMER,** author of *Solo in Salento: A Memoir* (Italian Translation: *Un'Americana in Salento*) and the Cat Gabbiano Mystery Series: *The Red Starfish* and *Moringa—Tree of Life*

"*Improvising in Italian* is a heartfelt memoir, unveiling the Italian world of food, art, vintage cars, and soccer teams, as well as the country's impenetrable bureaucracy. Throughout Jennifer Artley's courageous adventures and revelatory experiences, we grow alongside her as she poignantly grapples with and gains insight into the meaning of 'home.'"

—**ESTHER AMINI,** author of *Concealed*

"Having only fantasized about a life in Italy, I read this book largely to see if the reality lives up to the fantasy. It turns out that the answer is . . . depends on your fantasy. In this book, Artley does a masterful job of sharing an honest and humbling depiction of her move to Italy. The frustration in the antiquated systems, the total reliance on paperwork that will never be looked at, and the 'who-do-you-know' culture are juxtaposed with the warmth of the people, the exceptional quality and simplicity of the food, and the proximity to some of Europe's most desired destinations. But what I loved most about this book is the author's vulnerability in allowing us to see how far things fell from fantasy before she and her husband were able to find themselves . . . and the magic of Italy . . . again. It's a book about perspective as much as it is about marriage, self-awareness, and Italy, and it only made me want to go there more!"

—JESSICA GREENWOOD, author and ghostwriter

"Such a personal slice of a moment in time that left us all forever changed, through the eyes of a true nomad. A window into an incredible life of living everywhere, nowhere, and—for a moment—in Italy."

—ANDREW D. WELCH, author of *Field Blends*

Improvising in Italian

Improvising in Italian

by Jennifer Artley

© Copyright 2025 Jennifer Artley

ISBN 979-8-88824-623-8

All rights reserved. No part of this publication may be reproduced, stored in a retrieval system, or transmitted in any form or by any means—electronic, mechanical, photocopy, recording, or any other—except for brief quotations in printed reviews, without the prior written permission of the author.

Cover art and design by Lauren Sheldon

Published by

köehlerbooks™

3705 Shore Drive
Virginia Beach, VA 23455
800-435-4811
www.koehlerbooks.com

IMPROVISING IN ITALIAN

a memoir

JENNIFER ARTLEY

VIRGINIA BEACH
CAPE CHARLES

For Miko.

CONTENTS

Big Bang 1

Expand. 36

Collapse. 89

Big Crunch 133

Acknowledgments 171

BIG BANG

Chapter One

The first week we moved to Italy, my sixteen-year-old daughter, Julia, began having second thoughts. She said we could escape Italy together, like we had both been wanting to bust out of jail and my boyfriend, Michael, was the warden. She said we could go back to Hoboken, New Jersey, where we were living. She said it like it was as easy as turning the car around.

"Where would we live?" I asked. "We gave up our apartment."

"We could rent another apartment," she answered.

"What about all the things we gave away, like the TV, lamps, and kitchen appliances?" There was no point taking anything electrical to Italy since the European plugs and voltage would be incompatible.

"We could get new stuff," Julia said.

"What about Michael?" I asked.

"He'll be fine."

"What about John? He just moved to Amsterdam." John, her brother, was attending the University of Amsterdam. He was half the reason we had moved to Europe.

"He'll be fine too."

"What about Domo?" Domo was our dog, a terrier/basset hound mix I adopted after my divorce.

"He could come back with us," Julia answered.

I didn't say anything. I was quite certain Domo wouldn't want to get back on a plane.

There were a few issues going on. One was that Julia's ex-boyfriend (from Hoboken), who had broken up with her at the beginning of the summer, was now telling her he wanted her back. He knew perfectly well that she had moved to Italy. Two, she didn't like her new school. (We had done our research, but the reality of it, I supposed, was another thing.) Three, she concluded that Modena, a small tertiary city in the Emilia-Romagna region near Bologna, and the town we had chosen to live in was not going to offer her much. It was too dissimilar from Hoboken, where we had resided for four years, a dockside town that sat across the Hudson River from Manhattan and "*the sixth borough*" of New York City, some called it. Though, it was also a punchline for New Yorkers and historically home to infamous mobsters like Bobby Manna "Mots" Casella, and "Petey" Caporino.

"We can do it," Julia persisted. "You and I have always been a team."

"Exactly," I said. "We are a team. We need to stick it out together *here*."

"Why not in Hoboken? We were happy there."

"Yes, but we're here now. We all agreed to come *here*. We discussed it, remember?"

"I know, but I've changed my mind. I want to go back."

"Honey, it's not possible to go back now. I mean, where would we even go back *to*?"

"It *is* possible! Anything's possible," Julia stubbornly maintained.

While we were discussing the move to Italy, we reminisced about all the other places we had lived, and there had been many. "We've done crazier things," Julia pointed out, giggling. Like the time she and I went to Israel in 2012 after her dad and I separated. Shortly after we arrived, Israeli forces killed the military leader of Hamas, and Palestinian-armed groups in the Gaza Strip retaliated by firing missiles into Israel, the first time ever reaching Tel Aviv. Sirens blared, and everyone ran into bomb shelters while Israel's revolutionary rocket-defense system, the *Iron Dome*, shot down incoming missiles by Gaza militants. It wasn't funny, but the fact that I was in the middle of a very contentious divorce prompted us to roll on the floor laughing in hysterics at the ridiculousness of our situation.

"Honey," I said, taking a deep breath, "we just landed in Italy. We're all still acclimating. It's true we've had some . . . crazy experiences in the past, but you don't move to another continent to turn around and move back two weeks later," I said. I was pacing around our sauna-like apartment. It was August, and Italians didn't believe in air-conditioning. They complained it made their neck hurt. To escape the heat, everyone fled to the seaside, leaving Modena deserted and shut down like a nuclear apocalypse had occurred.

It didn't help that we had landed in a sparsely furnished apartment in a four-hundred-year-old building with dark hallways and a painfully slow elevator. Even the front door looked like something from two centuries ago that required a large metal key and five turns of the lock to open, in contrast to our three-bedroom apartment in Hoboken in a doorman building. I reminded myself that my mother once lived in a dingy apartment in Taipei to study Chinese. It was on the ground floor, had smelly toilet drains, and sat on a busy side street in Tien Mu. Like this apartment in Modena, it was temporary.

"But I hate it here," Julia said. "It's not a good place for me." She wouldn't let up.

"My love," I said, keeping my voice calm, "if it's any consolation, I also miss Hoboken." And I did. I chose to live there after my divorce. It reminded me of make-believe towns I'd seen in children's storybooks as a kid. The kind with big, colorful pictures of all the homes and businesses in town grouped together in a neat square: the church, the park, the grocery store, the butcher, the doctor's office, the hair salon, and then Main Street. Sitting along the Hudson River, it had a stunning view of New York City. At night, looking at the gorgeous lit-up Manhattan skyline, we could see the bright lights of the tall buildings: the Empire State Building, the Chrysler Building, and the Freedom Tower. We joked we had a far better view than those snobby Manhattanites on the other side of the river.

It was too expensive to live directly in Manhattan, so Hoboken, to me, was the next best place to be if you want to be a writer. I took writing classes at NYU and workshops in fiction, memoir, screenwriting, and playwriting. I joined writing groups and made friends with other writers. I went to readings and book signings and met famous authors. I was impressed with myself for doing things like going to the Village to take a film class. I was living a writer's dream.

Now, I was living the Italian dream—or struggling to, anyway.

"Look," I continued, "if you still hate living here in a few months, we'll move back, okay? Do we have a deal?" If she took me up on it, I'd have to honor the deal. But I was willing to do some serious negotiating.

"I don't know . . ." Julia shrugged. "I'm having a hard time adjusting to this country."

"But you've adjusted to other places," I said, flabbergasted that of all the places we lived, Italy was the one she couldn't tolerate.

"I'm sorry, but I can't this time."

After many exhausting discussions, I told Julia we'd at least *try* to live in Italy for a while, suffer through it as best we could. It would not only be wrong to go back—to give up after a few weeks—but it wasn't feasible either.

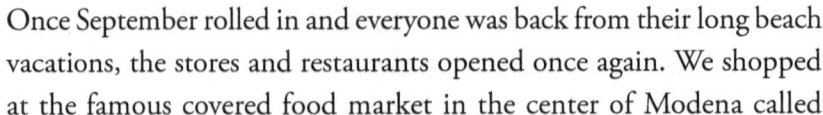

Once September rolled in and everyone was back from their long beach vacations, the stores and restaurants opened once again. We shopped at the famous covered food market in the center of Modena called

Mercato Albinelli, one of the oldest food markets in Italy that sold a beautiful variety of fresh produce, meats, fish, cheeses, and breads. We were surprised to see equine butchers. I read that Italy eats the highest amount of equine meat than any other nation in the world. It's a delicacy that dates to Roman times, and Italians rave of its health benefits. Julia and I tried it, but it felt sacrilegious.

"The animal died of natural causes," Michael said. Apparently, all the horses that were eaten in Italy died of natural causes, or so we were told.

We took walks around the Old City and discovered a small movie theater, museums, and an opera house. Along Modena's main boulevard, Via Emilia, we passed a full range of chic and fashionable boutiques with trendy clothes, several bookstores offering a limited selection of English-language literature, numerous fruit and vegetable stands, family-operated restaurants and cafés, as well as bakeries with the aroma of freshly baked bread wafting through the air. Via Emilia encapsulated the fundamentals of movement. It had originally been a Roman road used by pilgrims and goes in a straight line through the entire region of Emilia-Romagna. Modena, which sits along this ancient road, became the center of automotive design and achievement, known as the home to car manufacturers such as Ferrari, Maserati, Lamborghini, and Pagani. Their prototypes regularly zoomed by at criminally fast speeds, engines roaring with pompous elegance.

I was hoping that with school starting, having a regular routine, and Julia making new friends, she'd feel differently about Italy. But she was more determined than ever—she didn't want to be there. I desperately tried to talk her out of leaving, but one of the challenging things about being divorced when you have teenagers is that they have somewhere else to live: with their other parent. It greatly diminishes your parental power. And I suspected she felt guilty about not being near her dad too. He had been living in Seattle but moved to Maryland shortly before we left. I felt bad about that as well.

Yet, the main issue was that Julia felt trapped. When we took Domo for a walk in Parco Giardino Ducale Estense, we found out the park once had a zoo. Someone told us there had been lions there, and you could hear their lonely roars throughout the city. The thought of those poor, homesick caged lions roaring in sadness in the cold, foggy Modenese climate haunted me, and perhaps Julia could relate. She rebelled by not wanting to go to school. It wasn't like her at all; she had always been a good student. I found myself dragging her out of bed to get ready for class, which exploded into a screaming argument. Then, after a rushed breakfast, we dashed to our comically small, rented Fiat Panda parked outside the historic center (we didn't have a resident parking pass). We hopped in the car—or, rather, I hopped in, and Julia slumped in like a sloth—and then lurched into Modenese rush hour traffic and headed to her school in Montale. As other vehicles rumbled past, I navigated with a stick shift through narrow streets and countless roundabouts. I hadn't driven in months. In Hoboken, I only drove a few times a year.

When we finally reached the school, we'd jerk to a stop, and Julia would slowly melt out of the car. In the afternoon, I'd pick her up, and she'd sit miserably all the way home.

"You're experiencing culture shock," I said in the car coming home from school one day. "It happens to most people. It's normal."

"That's not it," she insisted. I kissed her head at a stoplight, knowing that adjusting to new places isn't easy, even for seasoned travelers like us. She had some amazing learning experiences in Hoboken, which taught her to be part of a community. She had volunteered at a day care for low-income families, making packed lunches every Friday for the local homeless shelter. She'd also been in local plays and musical performances and starred in a low-budget film. But she was ready to embark on a new adventure. Or so she had thought.

Perhaps moving from New York City to a small town in Italy was too big of a leap. *And yet*, Julia and I had taken much bigger leaps. When I was married to her father, our family moved six times, including from Toronto to Beijing.

When we first arrived in China, the company hired a realtor to show us houses to rent on the outskirts of Beijing in a town called Shunyi.

Our realtor was astonished that we had brought our dog to China. "You have dog?" she kept asking, as if we had been pulling her leg. We hadn't dared to mention we had a cat too. Her driver drove us around in a beat-up car while her two cell phones rang constantly. She was either calling someone or someone was calling her. Sometimes she talked into both phones at the same time as we were jammed in the small back seat with the windows down because there was no AC. For much of the day, we sat in bumper-to-bumper traffic while the car thrusted forward then stopped, then inched ahead, and then stopped again. When the driver would have any space on the road at all, he would zoom ahead, escaping several near collisions with pedestrians and bicycles to get a few spaces up. There was no barrier between us and the sound of the deafening traffic, the choking exhaust fumes, and the mixture of pungent smells of roasting meat, decaying vegetables, and urine. But at the end of the day, we did find a house in an expat compound that had a clubhouse with a pool. It was an oasis. A walled and protected enclave. But still, it was a leap.

I had been taking leaps my entire life. My parents were US diplomats, and we lived in South Korea, Nigeria, Israel, the Philippines, and Burma (now Myanmar). By the time I was six, I had already lived on three continents, been in two coups d'état, and flown from Minneapolis to London by myself. My mother would ask me then, "Do you like moving around so much?" How could I have answered that question honestly? I didn't know any differently. I suppose I didn't mind it. When I grew up, I married someone whose job required us to move frequently. I subjected my children to the same lifestyle, believing in the importance of having worldly experiences and hoping to instill a curiosity about other cultures.

With each move our family made, I promised the kids we would have a grand adventure and told them about the time my mother lived in Beijing in the nineties, and during my visits to her, she and I would search for Beijing's ancient beauty. We'd walk along sycamore-lined streets where old men sat on park benches with their caged pet birds. Sometimes we saw old Chinese women hobbling on bonded feet, and we'd peek into hutongs, the narrow alleyways where faded red gates offered a glimpse of ruined courtyard houses. The most special thing we did was visit the Ming Tombs in Changping Qu. We'd hike a short distance from the main renovated structures to the neglected areas, bringing packed lunches and eating on the crumbling steps of a deserted tomb, like travelers who just discovered an ancient place.

Years later, when I took John and Julia to the Ming Tombs, we arrived in a cloud of smog behind large tour buses as I asked our driver to find the deserted imperial tombs. We drove around the grounds but couldn't find the crumbling burial palaces anywhere, only the polished, over-renovated ones. We pulled over, got out of the car, and walked around aimlessly, hoping to locate this memory I swore I hadn't made up. It was a different place. It had changed.

Maybe it's easy to make promises—to yourself and to others—before you move somewhere new, when the dream of what could be feels reachable. Before we moved to Modena, I'd come for visits while Michael was setting up his business there. He was an investment banker and spearheading a project that involved purchasing Italian old-age homes. He assured me that it was a solid investment opportunity since Italy, per capita, had the second oldest population in the world (Japan had the first). His Italian business associate, Marco, would promise me that if I moved to Italy, Michael would buy me a new car, as if that's all that was needed to convince me.

"Ah-Jeni, would you like to own an Alfa Romeo Stelvio?" he asked me.

"Sure," I said, having only a vague idea of what Alfa Romeo cars were.

"Red or blue?" he'd ask as Michael looked at me and beamed.

"I'll take either."

"Maybe a red one," Marco had said.

It wasn't a promise of a new car that eventually got me to make the move; it was the promise of new experiences and possibilities. It was Italy!

I continued to hold firm with Julia that we were not going to move back to Hoboken so soon after we had arrived. We argued and cried, and Julia told me she wanted to live with her father in Maryland. It was not Hoboken, but at least it was on the East Coast of the United States, she said. Then finally, exhausted and defeated, I told her that if she wanted to live with her father, then I was not going to get in her way *if* she agreed to spend all her breaks, including Christmases and summers, with me. Michael, who had been pleading with Julia as well but had basically let me handle it, held me as I cried.

"What am I going to do without her?" I asked Michael, sobbing into his shoulder. "Once she leaves, we may never live under the same roof again!" Julia and I would lose precious time together—time we would never get back—and it was devastating. She was leaving home too soon.

"Pretend she's going to boarding school," Michael suggested. I thought this was a good idea. Many teenagers left home to go to boarding school. I had briefly gone to boarding school. But still, I didn't want her to leave. I loved her so very, very much! When the kids were little and I'd put them to bed, I'd kiss their little foreheads and say, "I love you, forever and ever, no matter what." I meant it, more than I had ever meant anything. Julia knew that my love was unconditional. Maybe this is why she felt safe enough to leave.

Even so, I thought about how I had lived in various countries with my mother when I was a kid—nothing as Western and picturesque as Italy—and I was pretty sure she would have never put up with me saying I was going to go live with my father. And yet, it appeared history was repeating itself: divorced mother taking daughter to live overseas and asking, "Do you like moving around so much?" It's a question only a mother feeling guilty would ask. Julia undoubtedly gave me her answer.

The night before Julia left to go back to the States, we slept in the same bed with our arms wrapped around each other. She was wedged next to me, her arms grasping my shoulders. I laid there in the dark, thinking about how she had always been my rock. I thought about that one awful night in Beijing, when her father and I had gotten in a fight and I had left the house in a fit of rage, slamming the front door on my way out, needing fresh air and distance from our place. I got on my bicycle and was about to take off when Julia, breathless, came running out of the house. Without a word, she hopped on the back of my bike, and together we rode off against the night sky, the streetlights blinding and bright. I steered through the dusty Chinese roads in a daze. Julia's little arms wrapped around my waist, holding on tight, gave me the only comfort I had in the world as tears rolled down my cheeks.

Though now I knew she was already seeing herself back in the States, like it was her refuge, and in the arms of her boyfriend, who was surely going to break her heart again. And maybe I had been equally naive. Maybe my visions were just as far-fetched and bound for disappointment.

The next morning, there was a steady stream of rain pouring down, and we dragged Julia's suitcase along the cobblestone street that was half-flooded. Occasionally, a car whooshed by and splashed our legs. We walked out of the historic center to a street outside its walls to meet Marco, Michael's business associate, who was waiting for us in his car. He had volunteered to drive us to the airport since the Fiat Panda was far too small for all of us and Julia's luggage.

Silently, we climbed into his car. Soon we were on the way, as the rain drummed steadily against the windshield, mixed with the sound of my sniffles and sobs. No one dared utter a word. And what could anyone say anyway? There were no words for this situation. None. Whatsoever.

When we got to the airport, we checked in Julia's luggage, though I was still hoping she would change her mind. We then walked her to security, hoping again she'd decide to stay. But no such luck. She was stubborn, and I supposed I had taught her to be that way. I had taught her to plow her own path, hadn't I? I had taught her to forge ahead when she knew what was best for her. That's what I did when I divorced her father. Now it was coming back around. It was karma.

I didn't want time to pass but to freeze long enough for us to reconsider, to stop and think about it for a while longer. But we found ourselves at the gates too soon, and this was where we had to say goodbye.

"Mommy," Julia said, and we threw our arms around each other, sobbing and making a scene. Then Julia pulled away, and Michael and I watched as she got in the security line, then disappeared. I was now, without any warning or preparation, an empty nester. *An empty nester.* It was frightening how fast things changed. How could I have ended up suddenly somewhere else entirely? *She is going to boarding school*, I repeated several times. *It's just boarding school.*

In my senior year of high school, I was sent to boarding school because my mother moved to Burma, where there was no accredited high school to attend. So, over winter break, twice a year for three years, I traveled to a place I could barely locate on a map. To get there, I'd fly through Tokyo, then to Bangkok, where I'd spend the night in the airport hotel. The next morning, I'd take another flight to Rangoon until, finally, I'd land onto a rutted tarmac next to a crumbling terminal building amid swaying palm trees in the hot dust. Rangoon was a decaying capital with mildewed Elizabethan-style architecture left over from the colonial period. It had lakes and parks and twisted old trees, and in the center was a golden-spired two-thousand-year-old Pagoda that loomed above everything. Outside of Rangoon, in the countryside, it was studded with pagodas and rice fields, farmers working the paddies in their conical straw hats next to their water buffalos, the scent of incense and jasmine in the air. It was a country that time seemed to have forgotten, and a traveler's dream, but not ideal for its citizens. General Ne Win ruled with an iron fist. Civil liberties were nonexistent, and the population lived in a state of fear.

This was where my mother lived. Burma was far from family and friends, far from my boarding school. And yet, when you're a minor, or in school, home is where your parents reside. In Julia's case, she had two options, Italy or Maryland, and she ultimately chose the latter.

The world was a smaller place than when I was a kid traveling with my parents to the far reaches of the planet. Now, we weren't so far away, having cell phones, the internet, laptop computers, and direct transatlantic flights. It wasn't like it was when I was a kid living overseas, when we communicated by letters, mostly, and rare telephone calls with bad connections. For me, fortunately, I could get to Julia in less than twenty-four hours if I had to.

After a while, when we knew there was no hope that Julia would change her mind, Michael and I walked out of the airport, emotionally drained. Feeling shaky, I allowed him to lead me into the parking lot where Marco was standing next to his car.

On the way home, I sobbed as the rain continued to pour down and the windshield wipers struggled to scrape away the water. Everything looked so gray and ugly and sad. This was supposed to be our family adventure in Europe, and this wasn't the scenario I had envisioned for us. I sat there in the back seat, shell-shocked, and reflected on the way things used to be before we moved to Italy. Had there been signs or clues that this would happen? Had I looked the other way? Now I was staring out the window into the fog, aware that I was in one of those surreal moments that would induce pain whenever I looked back on it. The understanding that the harsh realities of freeing ourselves forces others to change their lives, perhaps imprison them in a world they hadn't wanted. Which one of us was forcing the other to change their lives? Which one of us wanted to be free? We are interconnected, whether we want to be or not.

When we reached Modena, Marco stopped the car in front of the Old City, where he had picked us up a few hours before when I still had my daughter with me, and now she wasn't with us, and we opened the car door. I stepped a leg out into a puddle of water and got my shoes wet as Marco turned and looked at me, shaking his head. I was embarrassed that he had witnessed my deeply private family matter, something I wished I could have kept hidden. I had the urge to run, to get on a plane and follow Julia back to the States, but I froze, allowing the rain to pelt my legs like daggers. As I wallowed in my powerlessness, there was a part of me that admired Julia for being bold enough to take charge of her own destiny.

"Ah-Jeni," Marco said sadly as the rain poured down on the windshield, making the wipers thrash side to side. Perhaps he thought life would get difficult for him and Michael. If I was unhappy, I was sure he was thinking, it could disrupt business.

Michael stood outside holding an umbrella, looking like a blur through the window. Everything looked distorted. Instead of going back to the States, I was staying behind in *this*? How I wished I was more like my mother, who had been resolute, and Julia, her granddaughter.

I looked at Marco as he shrugged. "Ah-Jeni," he said again, "this is life."

I sighed as I got all the way out of the car and stood in the pouring rain. I didn't care that I was getting drenched. Everything I had known to be true had evaporated in an instant. I now couldn't remember why we were in Italy. I had taken a wrong turn. And yet, when I retraced my steps in my head, I had gone down the path I had *always* gone down. I had done what I had *always* done. Move. Start over. Adjust. Then leave. I was on a perpetual cycle of impermanence.

I didn't know how else to live.

Chapter Two

Once Julia arrived in the US, I called her numerous times to make sure she was okay. "How was your flight back?" I asked. "How is your new room at your dad's house? Are you getting enough to eat? When are you going to start your new school?" I worried she would be lonely, or she wouldn't find friends she'd have anything in common with. I worried she'd eat too much junk food, not get enough sleep, or think for even a nanosecond that I was mad at her or I'd hold a grudge. I was not mad, and I would never hold a grudge against her. "Mommy, I miss you," she said on the phone. "But I'm all right."

I stayed in bed for days and sobbed into my pillow while Michael tenderly brought me tea and coaxed me to eat like I was sick. He was a caregiver by nature. He was a Virgo, and his Life Path number was 6, all pointing to his nurturing tendencies. It was a great thing, indeed, to be the focus, or eye of desire, of such a nurturing person. I felt loved, warm, and safe, even if I was sad. At night, I stared at the ceiling and listened to Michael snore as our ancient building crept and rattled. The place felt haunted, and not with fourteenth-century ghosts but with my own.

Michael and I met when we were twelve. It was 1982, and we were in the same junior high class at the American International School in Kfar Shmaryahu outside of Tel Aviv. Our small class of twenty-five students were a tight bunch, and when we weren't trying to moonwalk to Michael Jackson songs or play spin the bottle, we went on school field trips to places like Mount Hermon in the Golan Heights, Jerusalem to see the Dome of the Rock, and the Negev Desert to ride camels and stay in a Bedouin tent. At some point, our class participated in an archaeological excavation at the Apollonia National Park, where we helped dig up crusader ruins dating back to the Phoenicians from the sixth century. I didn't know much about Michael then, even though we were close friends, and I don't think he knew that I had moved eight times already and lived in Israel when I was younger. He may have only vaguely known that my parents were divorced and foreign service officers, and my father lived in Prague.

Almost thirty years later, we reconnected on Facebook after the American International School of Tel Aviv organized a reunion. I didn't make it to the reunion, but Michael and I emailed for months, and we spoke on the phone. I learned that he still lived in Israel, worked in finance, was a father to three, played the guitar, and spoke three languages. I found his family background fascinating, which sounded like it had been taken from the pages of a historical novel. His family roots traced back to the ancient Silk Road that crisscrossed Persia, Afghanistan, and Bukhara, where his great-grandparents fled the Bolsheviks in the 1920s and then made their way to Mandatory Palestine (pre-state Israel) by camel and trucks through Iraq, Syria, and Jordan, with all their property stolen along the way. In the 1960s, his parents continued the tradition of the wandering Jew by living in Kobe, Japan, and then Milan, Italy, where Michael spent his formative years. His father was a gem merchant who traveled to Southeast Asia to collect rubies, emeralds, and jade. In the 1980s, the family moved to Israel and settled there permanently.

Michael didn't want to be a gem merchant like his father, so he got an MBA in finance. When he was done with school, he started working as a wealth manager for Prudential Securities, one of the Big Five Wall Street funds. He had to start at the bottom of the industry in sales, which reminded him of the Bob Dylan song "Subterranean Homesick Blues." "Twenty years of schoolin' and they put you on the day shift." His job was to bring clients to the firm, raise at least a million dollars, and convince people to trust their savings and 401Ks to a newly graduated rookie making $30,000 a year. Instead of cold-calling potential clients, like many of his colleagues, he targeted Israelis in high-tech development and went to seminars, networking events, and conventions. He raised $20 million for the firm in a matter of months. After that, Michael worked for various hedge funds, raising them capital too.

When Michael and I fell in love, being together seemed impossible. We were living in separate countries and had five kids between us. But our gut told us we were meant to be together.

"Maybe I'm a little crazy," Michael said one day on the phone, in the beginning stages of our relationship. "But for you, Jen, I'm willing to change the entire course of my life. I don't know how we can make it work for us, but we've got to figure it out somehow. Don't you agree?"

Michael hadn't moved as much as me, but he had also never found a place to call home. He was Jewish and had grown up in Italy and Israel, got a mostly American education, and had friends from around the world. He went to college in New York and became a naturalized American citizen. When he returned to Israel years later and decided to reside there again, everyone thought he was exactly where he should be. But in truth, he hadn't known where else to go. He was like the musicians he listened to, like Bob Dylan, Neil Young, Bob Marley, James Taylor, and the Grateful Dead, who all wrote about disempowerment and being far away from home. It wasn't a coincidence that he was drawn to those artists.

And yet Italy was where he recalled his best childhood memories.

"When I'm in Italy," Michael said on a vacation in Rome years before, "it instantly feels familiar. The sounds, smells, colors, sky. It's like putting on an old comfortable sweater."

"Tell me more," I said. It turned me on that he loved Italy and spoke Italian.

"Jennifer, *amore mio*," he said. Jennifer, my love. "*Quanto sei bella.*" You are so beautiful.

"Let's live in Italy someday," I said as I breathed in a sigh of contentment. "Okay?"

"Okay." He smiled.

"I mean it. Let's live here. Wouldn't it be wonderful?"

"That would," Michael said.

"As soon as we're able, let's travel back to Italy and drive through the countryside to pick the perfect spot to have a home." A warm feeling flowed through my body.

"I want a home with a vegetable garden," he said.

"I want to live in an Italian villa." I sighed.

In our delirious happiness, we wanted to stretch beyond the limits of what we thought capable, push boundaries, and go against the grain. Michael called this improvising. He said the Grateful Dead, his favorite band—part jazz, blues, bluegrass, country, and rock n' roll—improvised at their concerts.

"Listening to the Grateful Dead changed my life," he'd said. He explained that when he heard a recording of a live show at the Fillmore East from April 25, 1971, it changed his perspective of the world. Their live music was improvisational, and some of their songs went on for forty minutes. It was an invention of musical notes, an intentional dislocation from the world, moving the pieces around, never being the same. It was about living in the moment, on the edge. The long freeform instrumentals taught him to let life take him where it may. Like the Grateful Dead biographer, Dennis McNally, said, "Wholly committing to improvisation implies taking risks. It's a philosophy of leaving yourself open to possibility and therefore leaving yourself open to magic." Sometimes when you follow this path, improvisation will work, and sometimes it won't. But when you find the magic, it's worth it.

Michael understood my restlessness, but it was food that was the main theme in our relationship. Michael developed a penchant for strong flavors at age five. The first time he tasted black European licorice, he fell in love with it. He loved the spicy soy-flavored Japanese snacks and hummus and pita sandwiches with sliced Israeli pickles. At twenty, he stopped eating kosher when he first tried bacon and cursed out loud at its deliciousness. In his thirties, after his girls were born, he became particular about food quality and preparation and designated himself the main cook in the family. Then somewhere along the way, he became a bona fide coffee snob. In cafés, he was known to give explicit directions on exactly what temperature he wanted his cappuccino and the height of the froth.

When I was a kid, I was exposed to many different types of cuisines. My mother learned how to make bulgogi from my Korean nanny in Gwangju, and it became one of our favorite dishes. In Lagos, when I was five, I'd watch my Nigerian nanny pound a doughy mixture in a mortar in the servant's quarters behind our house. She'd scoop the mixture up in her hands, dip it in a sauce, and offer it to me. When we went to Greece on a family vacation when I was seven, I had moussaka. The savory combination of cinnamon, lamb, eggplant, and cheese was irresistible on my young palate. When my dad lived in Prague, in communist Czechoslovakia, he'd take me out to dinner, where the only items on the menu were schnitzel and fried cheese, which were savory and satisfying. When I visited my mother in Burma, we'd eat fried crab claws, giant prawns, curry and rice dishes, and mohinga, a bowl of noodles in a broth topped with condiments such as eggs, dried pepper, and dried fish.

Michael and I were obsessed with finding the perfect morsel in New York City: a piece of sushi, a well-constructed taco, a bowl of tortellini in broth, a crusty slice of rustic bread with soft butter and sea salt, and pizza Napoletana. We discovered Obika, a mozzarella bar in Midtown where we ate burrata for the first time. Takashi on Hudson Street in the Village was where we tasted real Japanese Wagyu beef. We frequented the Japanese restaurant Ootoya for yakitori and chirashi bowls. And we found a two-Michelin-star place on Seventh Avenue in the Village with some of the best sushi we had ever eaten.

In Italy, we loved the down-to-earth dishes made with fresh ingredients. Michael gave me a rundown on the formalities of Italian etiquette and food tradition. There were rules regarding eating that were considered important and taken seriously. Food rules were really the only rules Italians followed with strict precision and no messing around (the one exception was fashion). They never cut their pasta or used a spoon to eat spaghetti or ate pasta cold. Italians drank wine or water, and occasionally a beer at a pizza restaurant. In the mornings, they never drank a cappuccino after eleven, and they drank their coffee in a porcelain cup at a café or stood at a coffee bar, where they would drink an espresso or a café americano—which was an espresso diluted with hot water.

Michael taught me that different regions in Italy had their own signature dishes. The Emilia-Romagna region eats egg noodles and cornmeal and is known for stuffed pastas, mortadella, prosciutto ham, cotechino, risotto, pork byproducts galore, and *lardo*. Michael, who grew up kosher, explained that Italian lard is sliced from a pig's abdomen, then salted, spiced, and aged in marble for up to twelve months. It's mouthwateringly delicious.

Further south, from Rome and below, they eat durum wheat pasta and are known for dishes like carbonara, *cacio e pepe*, *carciofi alla giudia*, and fresh raw seafood platters, or *frutti de mare*, which is a delectable plate of raw shellfish like oysters, langoustines, and red shrimp, with only a squirt of lemon and a dab of olive oil to garnish. Napoli is known for its buffalo mozzarella and pizza. Always thin crust and the toppings simple, like fresh tomato sauce and mozzarella. All pizzas are personal size, never large pies.

We wasted no time visiting the local food artisans in Modena and the surrounding area and spoke with restaurateurs, local farmers, wine producers, and cheese makers. We tasted the varying ages of Parmigiano-Reggiano cheese from cheese mongers and went to *balsamico* vinegar shops and learned how *balsamico tradizionale* vinegar from Modena is a flavor enhancer, made from the byproduct of Lambrusco wine grapes fermented in barrels for twelve to twenty-five years, and known as "Modenese gold." In our kitchen cabinet, we had small flasks of homemade balsamico. In Modena, after a baby is born, the family starts to make the baby's own battery (or their own series of barrels) in their attics, where the temperatures in the winter and summer perfectly influence the fermentation of the bacteria. Our friends gave away their balsamico as gifts, and we used it on pasta dishes, bread, Parmigiano cheese, and in salads. We learned that there are health benefits to *balsamico*. It's good for your gut health, digestion, and overall immune function. In the eighteenth century, it was used as medicine and believed to be a remedy for the plague.

We befriended Gianluca, the owner of a gelato chain called Bloom. He was an articulate, tattoo covered jazz aficionado in his early thirties. His gelato was made with all natural ingredients, and his parlors had been given the honor of three cones, awarded by *Gambero Rosso*, which is the highest award a gelateria can earn. He got his inspiration from listening to musical artists like Miles Davis, he told us, and he often experimented with flavors. An example of one of his imaginative flavors was called "An American in Vignola Thinking About Milano." It was a bombshell combination of cherries, Campari liquor, and peanuts. We asked him how he came up with that idea, and he said he'd been walking with an American friend in a cherry field, picking cherries and eating them, and then they went for an *aperitivo* and drank Campari and munched on peanuts.

We also found a biodynamic farm operated by a man named Fregi who grew up in Brazil. He made a type of wine called *Pignoletto*, a white wine typical of the hills outside of Bologna, known locally as *I Colli Bolognesi*. Fregi showed us around his farm, explaining how, starting from the bacteria in the soil, everything on his farm worked in harmony. We listened to Fregi with great interest as we walked past a vineyard, goats feeding on the grass, a vegetable crop and a few pigs in a large fenced-in area with a view of the Apennine Mountains and the Italian countryside. I read in Dan Barber's *The Third Plate: Field Notes on the Future of Food* that organic fruits and vegetables contain between 10 and 50 percent more antioxidants than conventional produce. He also wrote that food is not only healthier grown from fertile soil, but it tastes better too. That also goes for the farm animals we consume that eat healthy grass and plants. Everyone wonders why Italy's food tastes so much better than the food in the United States. Here's one reason: they have healthier soil.

Seeing this farm made us think. We loved eating different cuisines, which we saw as another form of communication when traveling, a way to bond with people of different cultures. Like Anthony Bourdain said, "Food may not be the answer to world peace, but it's a start." We wanted to be open-minded and unrestricted. Yet there's the harsh reality of eating meat, industrialized farming, and its Holocaust-like cruelty toward animals. We decided we were going to be more conscientious about where our food is produced, no matter where we were living.

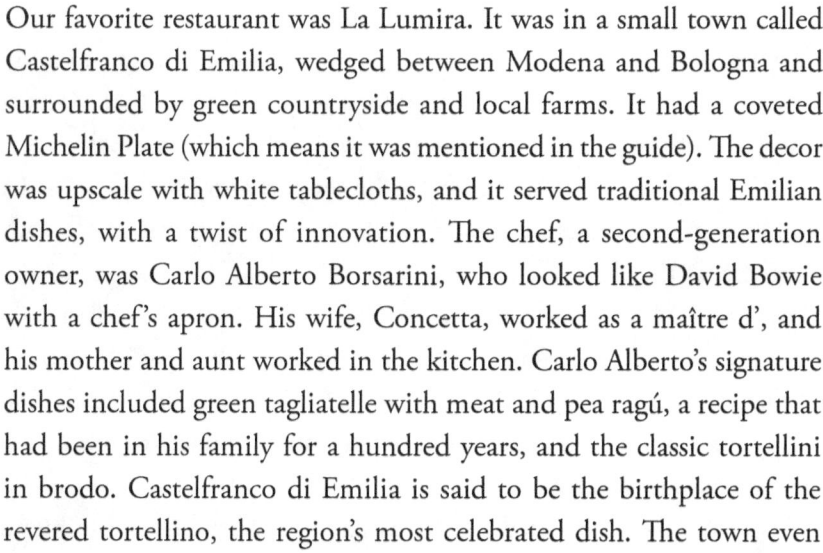

Our favorite restaurant was La Lumira. It was in a small town called Castelfranco di Emilia, wedged between Modena and Bologna and surrounded by green countryside and local farms. It had a coveted Michelin Plate (which means it was mentioned in the guide). The decor was upscale with white tablecloths, and it served traditional Emilian dishes, with a twist of innovation. The chef, a second-generation owner, was Carlo Alberto Borsarini, who looked like David Bowie with a chef's apron. His wife, Concetta, worked as a maître d', and his mother and aunt worked in the kitchen. Carlo Alberto's signature dishes included green tagliatelle with meat and pea ragú, a recipe that had been in his family for a hundred years, and the classic tortellini in brodo. Castelfranco di Emilia is said to be the birthplace of the revered tortellino, the region's most celebrated dish. The town even has a tortellino statue that stands in the central piazza on the main road. The word brodo means "rooster broth." Tortellino means "little pie," invented in the Middle Ages when peasants took leftover meat, folded it in pasta, and boiled it in the broth. It's one of those perfectly tasting dishes that satisfies the palate and is nourishing. For dessert, Carlo Alberto made several wonderful dishes, but we always ordered his homemade ice cream mixed with his own balsamic vinegar.

We befriended Carlo Alberto and once made the suggestion that he should conduct cooking classes for tourists. He wasn't interested, but we did collaborate on a couple of projects with him.

Michael arranged for Carlo Alberto to guest-chef at an upscale restaurant in Glastonbury, Connecticut. The idea came about when Michael's friend, Bill, an American restaurateur, visited Modena and we took him to La Lumeria for lunch. Bill was impressed with Carlo Alberto's food, and when he mentioned that his customers would love his dishes, Michael suggested that Carlo Alberto guest-chef at his restaurant. Bill thought this was a good idea, and so did Carlo Alberto. He had never been to the US and was curious to cook in an American kitchen.

Bill returned to Connecticut and planned the Italian extravaganza. For three nights, Carlo Alberto cooked a seven-course Italian dinner and dazzled the restaurant patrons with his signature, authentic family dishes. The experience was a cross-pollination experiment that Michael and I were hoping to repeat sometime with other Italian chefs.

On another occasion, we held a dinner party for sixty guests at La Lumeria with a traceable menu in which every dish was made with ingredients that had a direct link to local farms. We thought of the Slow Food Movement, founded in 1986, which germinated in Italy in response to the opening of a McDonald's near the Spanish Steps in Rome. The organization, which had grown internationally over the last thirty years, promoted a more healthy and slow approach to producing and consuming food.

Carlo Alberto decided that the main star of the traceable menu would be a tortellini in brodo, and he reconstructed the dish with all local and traceable ingredients, which included eggs, flour, meat, and cheese. Gianluca, the owner of the gelateria Bloom, whose gelato was made with all natural ingredients, provided the dessert on the menu. Fregi, the Brazilian biodynamic farmer, provided his biodynamic wine. Attendees of the event included the mayor of Bologna, some wealthy and locally known food connoisseurs, the press, and some local farmers who made speeches about the products they grew.

Then, of course, you can't mention Modena and Italian cuisine without mentioning the Michelin three-star restaurant Osteria Francescana and chef Massimo Bottura. In 2016 and then 2018, it was given the prize of the best restaurant in the world by the World's 50 Best Restaurants, claiming to be the authority in global gastronomy.

The restaurant, which sat on a narrow side street in the historic center of Modena, gained its first Michelin Star in 2002, the second in 2006, and the third in 2011. Three Michelin stars means "exceptional cuisine, worth a special journey." The Michelin Guide is the most revered culinary guide in the world, covering thirty territories on three continents. It made its start in France in 1900, when the Michelin tire company came up with the splendid idea of creating a guide that would motivate more people to drive to places and travel. Thus, in 1926, they rated restaurants, and the star rating was born. In the years that followed, and to date, anonymous Michelin Guide inspectors travel the world to rate restaurants, based mainly on their dishes, the service, and the atmosphere. They focus on quality of the ingredients, taste, consistency, value, and the chef's techniques and personality. Later, all the inspectors meet up and discuss their findings until they have rated each restaurant. The results are then published.

I first heard of Massimo Bottura in my Italian language class in Greenwich Village, where my classmates were middle-aged women planning to visit Italy someday. I mentioned I was moving to Modena, and one said in a heavy New York accent, "Have you seen *Chef's Table* on Netflix?"

"No," I said.

"You've got to see it," she said. "It's a new series about famous chefs. The first episode features a chef from Modena named Massimo Bottura. He has a restaurant there." When I told Michael about it, we watched the entire first season and talked about how we'd love to be the dinner guests of a Michelin three-star restaurant so we could taste the artistry and innovation of a renowned chef's molecular creations.

Shortly after we moved to Modena, we met Massimo Bottura and became friends with his American wife, Lara. Since we'd seen *Chef's Table*, we already knew that the couple met in New York City when they both were working at an Italian café. She was the barista, and he was in the kitchen. After several months of working together, Massimo went back to Italy, and Lara followed him there, giving up living in her home country forever. Later, they bought the restaurant that is now famous, got married, and have been together as husband and wife—and as business partners—ever since.

She gave us restaurant recommendations and tips on the best way to make a reservation at Osteria Francescana. During lunch one day, she told us about the Fini Hotel that was for sale. It had been a five-star luxury with a famous premier restaurant but had been closed for years. She said that Modena needed an upscale hotel, and their out-of-town guests normally stayed in Bologna, which was thirty minutes away by car.

When our lunch was finished, Lara told us how to get to the hotel, and we found it at the entrance of the Old City, abandoned in dust and neglect. It sat along a quiet cobblestoned street, with a flat roof and arched pillars in the front. The exterior was the color of faded orange and yellow, typical colors used in cities in the north of Italy. The windows were closed, with crumbling shutters. The building was like an aging actress who had lost her beauty and fame, still grasping at her rapidly disappearing youth.

Our imagination went wild with the idea of finding an investor and reopening the hotel and restaurant. Michael quickly secured us a tour after Marco introduced him to an architect who specialized in renovating old buildings. He had the keys and the plans and agreed to show us inside. He explained that the original owners made fresh pasta (in Modena, this mostly consists of tortellini and other stuffed pastas) and sold cold cuts (which are not the same as their North American cousin. In Italy, cold cuts are very much a delicacy). They also had a restaurant, which later became famous throughout Italy and beyond. In the late 1980s, Giorgio Fini, the original owners' son, sold the family's pasta and cold cuts to Kraft Foods and made a fortune. After Giorgio died, his son and daughter, Vittorio and Anna-Maria, took over the restaurant. Vittorio borrowed ten million euros from the bank to buy the building next to it so they could open a hotel. But the hotel business was badly planned from its inception. We heard they overspent and mismanaged the funds, and Vittorio never paid the bank back. The restaurant closed, and the bank took possession of the hotel, which sat empty ever since.

The architect led us through the hotel's elaborate door of dark, smooth wood and black iron castings and into the dusty lobby that had tall ceilings and a skylight that allowed a beam of sunlight to cast down on us as if we had walked upon a lonely stage. From there, we saw the front desk, a long, elegant staircase and banister, and an elevator. We then continued to follow the architect as he held the hotel's architectural plans in his hands, and we shuffled our way around the dark rooms with flashlights illuminating frescoes on the ceilings, marble and carpeted floors, and expensive cabinetry. The suites had luxury bathrooms with Jacuzzis and dark hardwood floors. There was one enormous suite that the architect proudly pointed out was where the pop star Sting had once stayed. Later, we walked through the massive restaurant and discovered that above the kitchen was a bakery. There was also a bar, spa, and banquet hall. The opulence of the hotel still showed through, the expression of the Finis' sybaritic vision. The place felt spectral, haunted by its history of glamour and unfortunate demise. While we paraded from one suite to another, through the dust of past decadence and fabled stories of guests such as the Shah of Persia and Ingrid Bergman, we snapped pictures for a future investor.

We imagined the hotel as a place of connection, where people from all over the world could meet—an opportunity for cross-pollination of ideas and passions. The hotel could display Italian art, have local musicians perform, invite local chefs, and showcase the local sports and car culture. We discussed how the red velvet carpeting should be ripped out, how the frescoes on the ceilings should be restored, and how the atmosphere should be made bright and airy and hip. I envisioned someone playing a piano near the staircase ascending to three-and-a-half floors of suites. We imagined every detail of what this place once had been and what it could be as I touched its surfaces and got its dust on my hands. I connected with this structure as if Michael and I were destined to bring it out of hibernation.

After the tour, we accompanied the architect to his office inside a sixteenth-century former grand palazzo with marble and frescoes, fountains, and a wide staircase. In his workspace, we stretched out the architectural plans on a wide table and went through each one, each floor, counting the rooms and suites, looking for doors, elevators, the restaurant, the bar, and the lobby. Michael and the architect spoke in Italian while I strained my ears for familiar words. We were excited about the prospect of making a positive impact on the little town we now resided in.

Chapter Three

No matter what our big plans were for Modena, we couldn't do anything in Italy without Marco, Michael's Italian business associate. In Italy, there's a saying: "*Fatta la legge trovato l'inganno.*" Loosely translated, it means, "No sooner is a law made than someone will find a way around it." This was part of the Italian culture of *clientelismo*, the basic tenet that you need contacts to function and navigate through Italy's notoriously complicated bureaucracy.

When we first discussed living in Italy, I wanted to live in Rome. I had only visited the Eternal City a couple of times, but to me, besides the sweltering summer heat, crowds of tourists, traffic, and pickpockets, it was enchanting. I loved the iconic ancient architecture and its "life is to be lived passionately" ethos.

"We can't live in Rome, honey," Michael said gently. Normally, he was open to my suggestions. We always encouraged each other, from where to live to career aspirations.

"Why not?"

"Because we don't have any connections there," he explained. "But I do have connections in Modena." He meant he had *a* connection in Modena, and that obvious person was Marco. He had already done a lot for us. He once arranged for us to have a private showing of the car collection owned by an octogenarian named Alberto Borghi, one of the most important classic car collectors in the world. He had 350 cars and motorcycles, including the first car built by Enzo Ferrari, the 1940 Auto Avio 815, as well as Benito Mussolini's private car, a 1929 Alfa Romeo 6C GT. After that, Marco finagled us a tour of the Pagani car factory, where they custom-made sports cars that sold between one and two million dollars, and we were guided around by Christopher, the son of founder Horacio Pagani.

Michael was a bona fide car guy. When Michael was a boy living in Milan, fast and beautiful automobiles were the preferred way of getting around the European continent, and the fastest, most beautiful, and sexiest cars were Italian. While my parents and I tootled around in a Volkswagen Bug, Michael was surrounded by Alfa Romeos, Lancias, Maseratis, and Ferraris. When he was a kid living in Milan, his family owned a bright orange Porsche 911 and a green Alfa Romeo Giulia GTV 2000. Every Sunday, his family, along with other Jewish families, would go to Monza Park, the largest walled park in Europe. Next to it was the famous Monza Racetrack, the home turf of Ferrari, and the venue of the Italian Formula 1 Grand Prix. In those days, cars—both race cars and street cars—were meant to be visceral and tactile. You could smell the gasoline. You could hear the differences in the engines. You saw them. You touched them. Cars were made to be memorable, individualistic, and original, with bold colors and designs, often the complete vision of one designer. They were artistic expressions that exuded a level of uninhibited jubilance, freethinking, and ingenuity. Not only that, but Italian car manufacturers were also killing it on the racetracks. The dominant driver at the time was Nikki Lauda for Ferrari. In 1976, he crashed his race car during a race, burning half his face off, but continued to race that season.

When Michael grew up, he read everything he could get his hands on about Italian classic cars, and as a result, he retained encyclopedic knowledge of Italian automotive design, engineering brilliance, racing, and production history. Because of him, I knew more about the subject than I ever cared to. Ironically, even though Michael once owned four Alfa

Romeos and a Lancia Delta Integrale (the holy grail for car collectors), we were now living in the Italian car capital of the world, renting a Fiat Panda, which was about as sexy as a Hello Kitty sweatshirt.

Marco also helped Michael get the temporary apartment we were currently living in. Plus, he helped us find a vet for Domo. Her name was Talita, and she made house calls. Marco found us a dog walker named Leopoldo, who happened to be the sweetest man alive. He loved clothes and had a particular obsession with designer bags and purses and promised to take me to Italian designer clothing outlets. Additionally, I hired him to help me learn Italian. We met in a café once a week and went over the conversational basics, and Leopoldo would fall over in his chair, laughing at my pronunciation mistakes. I am dyslexic and have never been good with languages.

"Ah-Jeni, honey," he'd say, wiping tears from his eyes, "you are so funny!" I smiled, thinking, *Where else can you find a dog walker/fashion consultant/Italian language teacher all in one?*

Marco had also introduced us to our vet's parents, Beppe and Antonella. Beppe was Sicilian, who had once been a professional soccer player but now worked as a soccer talent scout. Antonella was from Modena. The first time Antonella and I met, we set up a meeting at a coffee shop. She was a striking-looking woman with long silver hair. Her English was very good, except she often referred to things bluntly, which made me smile. For instance, instead of saying "breasts," she'd say, "the tits" without skipping a beat.

"I used to speak English much better when I was younger," Antonella told me. "I lived in England for a while."

"I love London," I said. "Julia wants to apply to universities there."

Antonella crinkled her nose. "I didn't like it. The English are mean. The German people are much more friendly. Very warm," she said. I nodded, but this left me wondering what kind of Germans she had met, as I come from German stock and Germans are not exactly known for their "warmth." Before she met Beppe, she explained, she went to Germany, planning to stay for two months, but she stayed a year.

There, she got a job as a runway model. We sipped espressos as she showed me pictures of her two grown daughters, and she told me about being married to a handsome, successful soccer player. Her husband, Beppe, had played for several top teams, the most important of which were Inter-Milan and Bologna, before ending his career at a premier football club in Indonesia.

I adored them both.

"Ah-Jeni," Beppe said one day, "Mike tells me you want to live in Rome."

"Yes," I answered. "I would have preferred Rome to Modena, to be honest." I felt I could be honest with him, but I was sure he would tell me that Modena was a fabulous place to live. Even though Palermo was where he was born and raised, he lived in Modena now to be near Antonella's family and their two daughters.

But instead, he said, "Jeni, listen very carefully. I am a Sicilian, and I will tell you the truth. Forget Rome. Tell Mike you want to live in Sicily." Beppe was supremely gifted at working the subject of Sicily into every conversation. "I know people in Palermo," Beppe continued. "I have connections there."

I nodded, wondering who these "connections" were, given he had family members in the Mafia. Michael had told me so.

"Let me explain something to you," he said, putting his arm around my shoulder. He lowered his voice. "Sicily is where you go to live, okay? You understand, Jeni? And Modena . . . well . . . it's where you go to die!"

Marco found us a furnished apartment in the historic center. It was under renovation and more expensive than what we wanted, but we were told it would be available soon. It was owned by a famous Italian soccer player, nicknamed Numero Uno, who was now retired, but when he played on the Italian national team, they won the World Cup in 2006. He was the fourth highest-scoring Italian player of all time.

He was also quite handsome.

When we toured the apartment, Numero Uno and his wife, a former model who was a puff of blond hair and makeup, gave us the grand tour. It had three bedrooms and two-and-a-half bathrooms on three floors, plus a huge kitchen. Michael and I didn't need so much space, especially since Julia was not living with us anymore (although when all the kids visited, it would be perfect). We noticed that none of the sinks in the kitchen or the bathrooms were installed, but, remarkably, large TVs had been mounted on the walls—four TVs, to be exact—and were adorned with heavy ornate frames like they were artistic masterpieces. Next to the TVs were gold leaf lamps that matched gold leaf ceiling chandeliers, along with purple velvet curtains in the master bedroom. It looked like the decorator was trying to be ostentatious and bored with the idea of mundane things like sinks.

The apartment, with all its space, was designed with no practicability in mind. For instance, the powder room downstairs was the size of a bedroom, but there was no coat or utility closet. In an apartment that could easily house six people, there was only one small shower in one of the bathrooms upstairs. The other full bathroom, decorated in black and gold tile, had a gigantic Jacuzzi tub equipped with disco lights that changed colors. There was also no laundry room. The laundry facilities were in the basement behind three locked doors, in what was supposed to be the storage room. The building was built in the fourteenth century, and the basement was creepy and dank. The lights were set on a timer and would automatically turn off every few minutes, leaving you standing in pitch darkness.

Still, it was either this apartment, or we risked not finding something else for a while. We were told that it wasn't easy finding apartments in the historic center. Michael and I discussed how the location was superb, how we'd have plenty of room for visiting guests and the kids, and we could invite people over for dinner parties. And though the decor didn't fit us at all, it would be kind of fun to live among impractical ostentation.

So, despite its obvious problems, we told Numero Uno and his wife we'd take it.

However, before we could sign the lease to the new apartment, I needed an Italian Tax ID number, or *codice fiscale*. Michael had already obtained his Tax ID from his past stays in Italy. I had to get it in the first month of my arrival, so we made an appointment at the Ministry of the Interior, or the *Agenzia delle Entrate*.

On the morning of our appointment, we got there extra early and joined the long line that had already formed outside the locked doors. When the doors were finally opened and our number was called, we sat down in front of a clerk. She had just begun her workday but looked like she was already longing for her coffee break. She gazed at us and sighed as Michael gave her the paperwork. She flipped through my passport and then looked up at us.

"Her Italian entry stamp is not here," she said to Michael in Italian. She explained that she needed to see this stamp as proof that I had entered the country within the month. She handed me back my passport and watched as we, confused and alarmed, flipped through it ourselves. She leaned on her elbows while looking amused by our efforts to locate this mystery stamp of mine. Several times, Michael and I carefully looked through my passport until we got to the end of the book. There was no Italian entry stamp for August. "Are you sure you entered Italy and not another EU country?" the clerk asked me.

"Yes, I'm sure," I said.

Michael explained that I had flown into Milan in August with him, my daughter, Julia, and our dog. He told her that our dog's entry into the country had been thoroughly documented.

At the airport in Milan, after we went through immigration, we were told to pick Domo up at the cargo building. It was a separate structure next to the airport, and we had to present his paperwork to three different offices to get our dog released. We had a letter from the Veterinary Association of New Jersey stating that he was healthy and fit for travel. We also handed over his vaccination records and pet passport. At each office, the officials meticulously went through Domo's papers and made photocopies of everything. Each official then handed the papers back and directed us to the next place to stand in line, until finally, in the third office, the official filed Domo's papers into a cabinet with endless files of other dogs that would never be looked at in a million years. But *my* passport hadn't been stamped!

"What is Jennifer supposed to do?" Michael asked the clerk impatiently.

"Exit the Schengen Zone and come back?" she suggested, shrugging. "Or go to the Questura in Modena and show them your plane ticket. Then they'll stamp your passport." The Questura was the immigration office. The latter was a much better and less costly idea.

Michael called Marco and told him what happened. Marco said he would make some phone calls. Some of the immigration officers at the Questura were his old-school buddies. He called back minutes later and said he was able to get us an appointment within the hour. This was why we had come to Modena and not another Italian town, Michael reminded me.

"Imagine doing this in Rome," he said. Now I understood the value of being in Modena, and I had a newfound appreciation for the *clientelismo* culture. We hadn't lived in Italy for more than a few weeks, and we were already taking clear advantage of this loophole.

The Questura was in a plain industrial-looking building on the edge of the city. The waiting room, which had no apparent ventilation system, was grim and full of bored-looking occupants. Fortunately, we skipped the line and were taken through the back door, otherwise known as the "friends and family" entrance, where we bypassed weeks of bureaucratic folly and entered an office. The immigration officers were sitting at their desks and looked up at us. They were wearing tight blue shirts and pants and shiny shoes with no socks. They had tanned skin, black gelled hair, and finely groomed long sideburns. It looked as if we had walked into an office of men about to pose for next year's "sexy immigration police" calendar, and I thought American immigration officers could stand to take some fashion tips from them. One of the officers looked through my passport and checked his computer. I was not in the system. So not only had my passport not been stamped, but it hadn't been scanned either. There was no official proof I was in the country, or, for that matter, in the EU. I had even gone to Amsterdam and back.

When we first arrived in Italy, Julia and I flew to Amsterdam to see John so he could give us a tour of the university and his new city. In the span of a few days, we walked along quaint and bustling streets lined with tall, narrow houses and canals with Dutch names like Brouwersgracht and Amstelveenseweg. We passed Indonesian restaurants, frits (delicious Dutch-style french fries), and pickled herring stands. We went to the Van Gogh Museum and the Anne Frank House, where we strolled through silently, tears in our eyes, flabbergasted, reminded of how horribly humans can treat each other. Now I realized that all along not one EU official knew I was in Europe.

In the Questura, I handed over my plane ticket to an immigration officer who did not reveal any embarrassment over the fact that a foreigner had slipped into the country undetected, never mind the EU and Schengen area. There was no "Oh, *scusi, signora*! Sorry for your inconvenience!" Instead, they directed me to a little photo booth outside the building and told me to get my picture taken. Then, I needed to come back to the office to fill out paperwork.

"Let me get this straight," I said to Michael, thoroughly irritated. "When you fly into the country, you get your passport scanned. *But* if an immigration officer forgets to scan your passport, when that is their primary function, you must fix their mistake by getting photographed?" I didn't understand how my passport's photo wasn't sufficient. They had already photocopied that, of course.

"I guess so."

"*Then* you must spend hours filling out paperwork?"

"It looks that way."

"Sheesh!" I wondered what it was about bureaucracies and their love for paperwork. It had to do something with the appearance that things were getting accomplished, when, in fact, piles of paper clogged up and covered up inefficient systems. Italy wasn't exactly savvy to the ways of the modern age. They were archaic when it came to this stuff.

When I was done with the forms, the immigration officer stapled my photo and papers together, gave them one more stamp for good measure, and shoved them into a drawer. Now my paperwork was stashed in an Italian immigration office in Modena, like Domo's in the airport.

With my hard-earned Italian Tax ID, we signed the apartment lease. Our sofa was in the building's entryway because it was too big to bring up the stairs. Numero Uno said they'd have to get a crane to lift it through the kitchen window. Of course, getting a crane to the historic center had to be approved by the city and would require paperwork . . . and weeks of waiting.

"Whatever," we said, "we'll live without a sofa for a while."

But then we noticed the refrigerator was not hooked up. Neither were the washer and dryer. The appliances didn't even have the proper plugs. We found a Home Depot-like store and bought and installed them ourselves.

But *whatever*. We were happy to be in our new, enormous, ostentatious apartment.

We could finally settle into our new life.

EXPAND

Chapter Four

Every morning, we'd wake up to the sound of church bells as the sun broke out over the tiled roofs and shimmered its golden light on the old township. We were getting used to living in Numero Uno's apartment and beginning to appreciate the disco lights Jacuzzi and large TVs. We spent most of our time in the kitchen, which was cheerful and bright and overlooked a lively street full of bars and restaurants. I also spent time on the third-floor loft, which had a small balcony with a view of the tiled roofs of the city center and the towering Ghirlandina. I used this room to write. On my breaks, I'd go on the terrace, look out, and listen to the disembodied voices that belonged to the townspeople below.

Before lunch, most days, Michael and I would go to Mercato Albinelli, where we'd approach the vegetable and fruit stands that had a choice assortment of tomatoes, blood oranges, white asparagus, spinach, *songino* (small dark green leaves to put in salads), and broccoli rabe. Then we would go to the cheese counter and buy *stracchino*, a soft cow's milk cheese that's slightly bitter, or *primosale*, a fresh young cheese that you can slice. After that, we'd go to the meat counter and ask for the little rabbit sausages, perhaps? We'd walk home to our apartment, and Michael would whip up a lunch of rabbit sausages and serve it with roasted potatoes, a green salad, and sliced tomatoes, called *cuore di bue*, meaning oxen heart, with a drizzle of olive oil and a sprinkle of salt. We'd eat ripe figs for dessert, washing it down with a bottle of Lambrusco wine.

Michael and I were making friends. We met a couple named Abbie and Andrea. She was from Australia, and he was Italian. They were purveyors of fine foods and owned a coffee shop in Modena. As soon as Michael and I met them, the four of us burst into conversation with hardly a breath in between sentences. They told us how they met in Hong Kong, got married in Italy, moved to London, and then decided to move to Modena since they had family there, but they were now setting their sights on Asia again, thinking of Singapore, or maybe Dubai. Since food and travel were their obsessions, we were over the moon to have met them.

I had also made friends with an American woman from California named Piera, an acupuncturist who studied Chinese medicine and taught yoga. My other American friend was Wayne. He was in his seventies and came to Italy several decades before when he fell in love with an Italian man. Now he was living with a thirty-five-year-old Egyptian who had run away from Egypt to escape his military duty. Wayne's apartment was in an ancient building in the center of the Old City. It had high ceilings, frescoes, velvet, oil paintings, enormous chandeliers, and marbled statues. It was like walking into the chambers of Marie Antoinette.

Many of our new friends were Italian, some married to foreigners. They were lawyers, translators, art dealers, entrepreneurs, and journalists. This included an Italian entrepreneur named Enrico who we felt close to as soon as we met, like we had reunited with a long-lost brother. He and Michael had different backgrounds but could relate to each other in their work and family dynamics. He was married to Courtney from Alabama. She moved to the UK twenty years prior, after she graduated from college, to be a journalist. She now worked for the *Financial Times* in London, her area of expertise in Slavic countries.

She even hosted her bachelorette party in Ukraine. She was smart, funny, lived life to the fullest, and resided in both London and Modena with her handsome Italian husband. I admired her like one admires Diane Sawyer. I was in awe of all her accomplishments.

Enrico's great-grandfather was a wealthy industrialist and the head of the Fascist Party of Modena when Mussolini was in power, and his other great-grandfather was a Jewish lawyer who escaped Italy during World War II.

"That makes me part Jewish," Enrico said proudly one night. He often wore a sports coat, with a handkerchief peeking out of the pocket, and slacks and impeccable shoes. He was the epitome of the way Italian men dressed, which I appreciated. I loved how Italian men took fashion seriously and weren't afraid to wear bright colors. In New York, if we saw a man wearing pink with a scarf thrown around his neck, we'd say, "If he's not gay, he's European."

He was raised Catholic but explained that one of his cousins decided to go back to his Jewish roots and become religious. "My cousin celebrates the Jewish holidays like Yom Kippur," he said. "You know that holiday where you starve yourself for three days?" Sometimes he wouldn't know the right word in English.

"Fasting," Michael said. "It's called fasting."

Modena had a 150-year-old synagogue in the Piazza Giuseppe Mazzini, which had once been a Jewish ghetto, but now the Jewish community was so small, the synagogue did not have enough members to form a quorum. Jews had been in Italy for over two thousand years. In 1516, Venice began making it obligatory for Jews to live in a walled-off area with guarded gateways and enforced curfew. The practice of isolating Jews in ghettos spread to other Italian cities, including Modena. The ghettos were abolished in 1859 after King Victor Emmanuel II unified Italy and granted equal rights to Jews. But his son, King Emmanuel III, appointed Benito Mussolini, who was the leader of the Italian Fascist Party and admired by Adolph Hitler, as prime minister in October 1922, and Jews began to be targeted once again.

If you've seen old films of Benito Mussolini, you'll have noticed that he was aberrant, a colorful tyrant with an impressive physique, who stuck out his chest when he walked and spoke with dramatic and theatrical hand gestures. He loved violence and bragged about it. His cultish thugs, called the Blackshirts, were armed squads of Fascist loyalists who terrorized the population in their search for socialists, communists, or anti-fascists. They committed all manner of crimes against their fellow Italians and with minimal interference from the police or military. Their ideology required blind loyalty. Anything that opposed the state would not be tolerated. That went for anyone who did not go along with the narrative or was seen as disruptive to the cause. And—it should be noted—fascists did not have the same love of food that Italians have today. Mussolini and his goons ate for sustenance only, and on the go.

After Hitler came to power in 1933, anti-Semitism appeared in Fascist newspapers accusing Jews of wanting to conquer the world, and Mussolini began saying that Jews were internationalists, people with dual loyalties, and asked them to choose between Zionism and Fascism (though he never really gave them the choice). He spoke of a "Jewish problem" in Italy, and fascists began claiming that Jews were racially different from Italians. They referred to *The Manifest of Race*, which said that the people of present-day Italy were of Aryan origin. It proclaimed that Jews did not belong to the Italian Race, and additionally, whoever called himself a Zionist had no right to try to retain obligations, honors, or benefits in Italy.

In 1938, Italy enacted the Jewish Racial Laws. Jews were not allowed to be teachers, journalists, bankers, or members of the Fascist Party (up until that point, Jews could and did join the Fascist Party). Among other restrictions, they were forbidden from working as a peddler, in the music industry, or in the theater. They also could not sell used items, own a radio, register themselves in a phone book, raise horses, post death notices, or sell land. Basically, they could do nothing to earn money or function in society. Italy joined the Axis powers in 1939, declared war on Britain and France, and entered WWII as Germany's ally.

Enrico's great-grandfather, who was the wealthy industrialist, was ousted from the Fascist Party for questioning Italy's military readiness to join the war and Mussolini's bond with Hitler. He did not believe Jews were a danger to the state. Meanwhile, Enrico's Jewish great-grandfather heard reports of Jews being transported by trains in Germany and decided that he and his family needed to leave Italy. So, in 1942, they escaped to Argentina. Good thing, since 8,000 Jews were deported from Italy and murdered in Nazi extermination camps.

In July 1943, Mussolini, who had brought Italy to the brink of military disaster, fell from power when he was voted out by his own Grand Council. The Italians were losing the war, and they were left with two choices: continue fighting with Germany or surrender to the Allies. They decided to pull the "ole' switcheroo". They joined the Allied forces and declared war on Germany. They told their soldiers not to kill *those* guys anymore but *those* other guys instead. Italy already had a reputation of a disorganized military; I can only imagine the confusion.

However, Italian partisans, underground anti-Fascist guerrilla fighters, were helping the Allied forces fight the Germans and Mussolini's government. The Allied forces had invaded Sicily and then moved up the mainland and crossed over to the borders of Northern Italy and fought in the area around Modena. At the end of April 1945, the Allied forces managed to push the German troops out of Italy, and they took control of the country. In the meantime, Mussolini, the now deposed former dictator, and his mistress, Clara Petacci, tried to escape to Switzerland, but they were captured and shot by Italian partisans. Their bodies were taken to Milan and hung upside down in the square called Piazzale Loreto, where an angry mob assaulted the corpses.

After the war, Victor Emmanuel III abdicated the throne, and his son Umberto II reigned for only thirty-four days until the Italians voted for a republic, and parliament kicked the royal male heirs out of the country and banned them from ever returning. The ousted royal family went to Switzerland and lived the life of luxury among the rich and famous in Geneva.

In 1997, in a television interview, Umberto II's son, Prince Vittorio Emanuele said that Mussolini's racial laws were "not so bad." In the meantime, his handsome son, Prince Emmanuel Filiberto worked as a hedge fund manager for a bank in Geneva, and in his free time, starred in commercials and reality dance shows. In 2002, the Italian Parliament thought the ousted family had suffered enough and ended the ban on them. The royal family returned to Italy.

The war was now long over, however, and Italy was friendly to Jews and immigrants. Michael and I felt welcomed, and we began hosting dinner parties. Our kitchen was equipped for preparing large meals because Italian kitchens, though typically smaller than American kitchens, were designed to cook in. One of the few times we tried to host a dinner party in Hoboken, Michael set off the oversensitive smoke detector that was stupidly located directly above the stove in a windowless kitchen (you'll rarely see a windowless kitchen in Italy). The entire building was evacuated, and within minutes, three siren-blaring firetrucks pulled up, and suddenly our apartment was filled with ax-wielding firemen dressed in their full firefighting regalia. That was the last time we tried to cook a meal for more than four people there.

After dinner one night in our apartment in Modena, we took our guests up to the loft with the terrace so we could gaze at the tops of the tiled rooftops. We all clamored up the steps and threw open the terrace doors, where we were instantly enveloped under the star-filled night sky. We gazed out at the rooftops and pointed at the fourteenth-century buildings illuminated along the narrow streets. I grabbed Michael's arm and squeezed it, swept up in the magic of Italy. I felt a rush of happiness, which I hadn't felt since John had visited. As we stood on the terrace, Enrico told us his family owned a castle.

The next day, a group of us drove to the medieval castle called Monfestino toward the Apennine Mountains. It was a beautiful cold day, and we caravanned up to the top of a mountain, where the fortress was located. Enrico proudly gave us a tour of the castle and the grounds as he described how his great-grandfather, the wealthy Fascist industrialist, had purchased the eleventh-century fortress in the early 1900s. Then he had it restored and made into a residence for himself. We climbed one of its towers and gazed out across the valley, breathing in the cool and refreshing mountain air. At the end of the day, we took pictures with our arms around each other like we've been friends for years, the castle's turrets and the Emilian countryside as our backdrop.

There was much to be grateful for. Julia and John would be in Italy for Christmas. Michael had found a potential investor from London interested in the Fini Hotel. They had been talking about the hotel's history, its potential, and the cost of hiring a management company. I was adjusting to my life in Italy. My new friends were making this transition much easier.

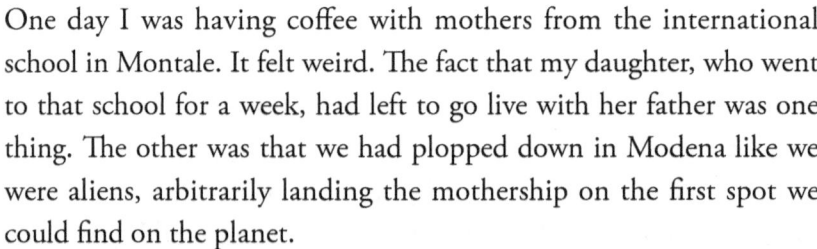

One day I was having coffee with mothers from the international school in Montale. It felt weird. The fact that my daughter, who went to that school for a week, had left to go live with her father was one thing. The other was that we had plopped down in Modena like we were aliens, arbitrarily landing the mothership on the first spot we could find on the planet.

"Who does your husband work for?" an American woman from the group asked me. She was beautiful and wore a blue dress and heels. American women living in Italy dressed well, I noted. I was no exception. When I arrived in Modena, I had long, dark, straight hair, and I often wore jeans and peasant tops. Now my hair was shoulder-length, layered, and almost blond, and, on that day, I was wearing slacks, a fitted blouse, and suede flats.

"Uh . . ." I hesitated.

The woman assumed my job didn't bring us to Modena since I was having coffee with the group on a weekday. And I didn't bother to correct her that Michael and I weren't married. I didn't know how to explain what Michael did or his old-age home deal, which was trudging along but not moving nearly as quickly as it was supposed to. The SGR (a Bank of Italy regulated entity) in Rome, a fund for foreign investments, was refusing to bring in any equity investors like they said they would. They wanted Michael to do all the work by bringing in the equity *and* finding all the old-age homes. I could see that Michael was getting stressed about it.

The American woman began listing all the companies and industries in Modena that had foreign employees, as if I was being difficult about answering the question about what my husband did for a living and why we were living in Modena.

"Does your husband work for Ferrari?" she asked me.

"No."

"Maserati?"

"No."

"The tile industry?"

"No."

"The food industry?"

"No."

"Tetrapak?" (That's a Swedish company).

"No. None of those," I said.

"Do you have family here?" a woman from Germany asked.

"No."

"No family?" The conversation was like playing twenty questions, trying to guess who Michael and I were and what we did. It was unheard of to randomly move to Modena. Michael and I hadn't moved there randomly, but it certainly looked that way. We were doing everything backward too. Our visa issues were looming over our heads. I still had a tourist visa, and I was supposed to leave the Schengen Zone every three months. I'd fly to London, Dublin, or the United States to visit Julia. Then I'd come back a week or two later, and we were sure nobody would enforce the rule that I was technically supposed to stay out of the country for three months. Heck, they didn't even know I was there until I told them. Michael was being sponsored by an Italian company (through connections), but he still needed to get his EU Blue Card, or he wouldn't be able to work in the country legally.

"We're . . . um . . . free agents," I said. I didn't know how else to explain it.

"Free agents?"

"We came here on our own," I clarified.

"Hmmm . . . " a Swedish woman uttered and took a sip of coffee. This woman had lectured me about how I needed to get my Italian driver's license. She told me I'd first need to hire a tutor to help me study for the written driver's test since there were 4,000 driving rules. And, before I took the written test, I'd need to have a good handle on Italian; you couldn't take it in English. Then, just to make it extra difficult, it was required that they test your ability to drive in a car with a stick shift, though getting a driver's license wouldn't become an issue until I was technically an Italian resident. In the meantime, I had an international driver's license, which was easily obtained at an AAA (American Automobile Association) office in the States. All that was required was a valid license and thirty dollars.

"Is your husband Italian?" a British woman asked.

"Michael lived in Milan when he was a kid," I said, "but . . . uh . . . no." His family never acquired Italian citizenship. His grandparents lived in Milan for over sixty years, died there, and yet, they never became Italian citizens. Michael told me that this not getting citizenship thing was a strange habit of the wandering Jew. "There's an unwritten rule," he said once. "Always stay separate and apart from your hosts." In other words, remain on the outside. I was used to being on the outside; that's where I had always been anyway.

"So, you guys just showed up in Italy? Just like that?" the American woman asked. She was very persistent.

"Well—"

"Then why *on earth* did you choose Modena?" This was what everyone wanted to know.

"We have a connection here," I said.

"A connection?"

"You know, to get things done when dealing with the bureaucracy and stuff. He's a business associate of Michael's." Their eyes glazed over. Clearly, they were not familiar with the *clientelismo* culture. They didn't have to be. Their companies handled everything.

"Ah," an Austrian woman said, "so your husband works here on his own, and you're . . . ?"

"I'm writing a book," I said.

I didn't bother to explain that I was living off my divorce settlement or that we were looking to be involved in the Fini Hotel's reconstruction and opening. It would be far too complicated to explain.

This line of questioning reminded me of high school in Northern Virginia, after we came back from being overseas. I felt different being in a school with students who had known each other since kindergarten. The kids at my new school questioned me about where I was from, and I didn't know how to answer that simple question. In terms of home, the closest thing was Iowa, since that's where my parents grew up and where both sets of my grandparents lived. The family farm had a meadow with cottonwood, walnut trees, and a winding creek on the edge of a field of rustling corn. I spent my summers playing with my cousins, being the strange one from Nigeria, Israel, the Philippines, or whatever country I'd been living in. Yet Iowa was a place I only knew in the summer, when life was carefree, warm, with no routine. I didn't know it completely. I was an outsider there too.

In my high school in Northern Virginia, I felt adrift. It took me a while to adjust and make friends. Yet, in a world where everyone was characterized and stereotyped, I refused to be labeled and didn't identify with any group. While it pained me that I wasn't like my peers—I was never going to be someone they knew since kindergarten—I also rebelled at the idea of being molded into something that wasn't me.

However, these women, the mothers, were friendly and wanted to be helpful. I appreciated them including me in their group, even though I was an empty nester now. They were sympathetic and sweet about it.

"Do you know there's a world-famous restaurant right here in Modena?" the American woman asked me later.

I nodded.

She mentioned Massimo Bottura and then said, "His wife's name is Lisa, I think. I can't remember."

I kept quiet. Not only had Lara come to our house for dinner several times, we had gone to the restaurant already, and she practically treated us like private guests.

On the night of our reservation, we felt fortunate that we were trotting off to the number-one restaurant in the world. The entire experience was perfectly choreographed: taking our coats, being seated (there were only twelve tables in total), and being served. The waiters moved around effortlessly, filling water glasses and bringing our dishes, which came at a perfect pace.

The most iconic dish was *Five Ages of Parmigiano-Reggiano in Different Textures and Temperatures.* It was twenty years in the making. Lara had explained that it was quite innovative. Parmigiano-Reggiano cheese was presented in five different ways: a soufflé made with twenty-four-month aged Parmigiano-Reggiano, a mousse made with thirty-month-aged Parmigiano-Reggiano, a creamy sauce made with thirty-six-month-aged Parmigiano-Reggiano, a crisp wafer that was made with forty-month-aged Parmigiano-Reggiano, and froth from a broth made with fifty-month-aged Parmigiano-Reggiano. This was an extremely rich and decadent dish, the way butter or Wagyu beef feels to the palate.

It took three hours to devour our gluttonous entrées. The bill for two at Osteria Francescana could give you a small heart attack, but unbeknown to us, Lara had instructed her staff to slash our bill in half, which we only noticed when we got home, because in a Michelin three-star restaurant, when presented with the bill, you don't look at it; you just sign and walk out. When we left, we were giddy and excited and recounted our favorite dishes like people recount their favorite scenes in a movie.

But from the point of view of the mothers of the Montale school, Michael and I had just materialized in Italy; we seemed lost. We didn't know how to obtain an Italian driver's license, and I was still there on a tourist visa. So, I wasn't about to tell the Montale mothers that we had somehow already figured out how to get a table at Osteria Francescana, where there is normally a six-month waiting list. It said something about our priorities. Thinking about this, I realized we were not much different than our new apartment. Full of bells and whistles but not the practical stuff.

Chapter Five

We were excited that Michael had found an investor for the Fini Hotel, but when he went to talk to the bank president, from the bank who owned the nonperforming loan on the hotel, he felt discouraged. The bank president wanted to sell the hotel for three times its value, and he also wanted a bribe. The bank had lent Vittorio Fini the money to buy the hotel, which created the financial hole that then led to the hotel bankruptcy, and now the bank wanted a payoff?

"There's a saying in Hebrew," Michael said, "that means you have murdered a man and inherited his property too." Michael was known to pepper his sentences with proverbs and colorful curse words. Although somehow the proverbs were always in Hebrew and of biblical nature, the swear words were always in Italian.

"Is the investor going to give him a bribe?" I asked.

"Of course not."

"What are you going to do then?" I asked.

"Wait for it to go to auction," Michael said. "We're not going to pay what the bank wants, and we're not going to pay off the bank president either."

It hadn't occurred to me before that the bank would risk losing an investor, gamble, or act unprofessionally. It was a major bank after all.

"What happens at the auction?" I asked. "What if somebody

else buys it?"

"Nobody is going to buy it at the first auction," Michael said. "Everyone will wait for the second auction to see how far the price will go down. It's likely there will be a third auction or fourth, even."

"You're not worried that somebody else will come along?"

Michael looked at me pointedly. "Listen, the hotel has been sitting there for the better part of a decade, and nobody has paid any attention to it. The bank will be lucky to get a couple million for it around here."

Yet when auction day arrived, a buyer swooped the hotel up at full price. We were baffled and confused. If things had operated the way it was supposed to, there would have been a second auction, maybe a third. The rumor was that the buyer had borrowed the money from the same bank that had the nonperforming loan on the hotel and had used that money to buy the Fini Hotel to cover up the bank's first failed loan. Maybe that was true, maybe it wasn't, but it suddenly became clear that we never had a chance in hell.

"Marco said the building has bad mojo anyway," Michael said, as if wanting to not care what happened. I didn't remember him saying that, although I had remembered him saying he thought it was a mistake for us to get involved with the hotel in the first place. I thought he didn't want Michael to lose focus on their business of investing in Italian assisted-living homes.

"I hope the new owner does all those things we talked about," I said. "Modernize it. Open the restaurant."

"It's out of our hands now," Michael said.

It was done. There was nothing left for us to do.

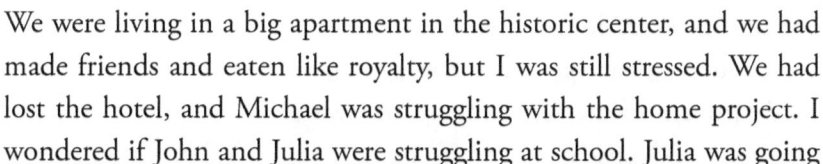

We were living in a big apartment in the historic center, and we had made friends and eaten like royalty, but I was still stressed. We had lost the hotel, and Michael was struggling with the home project. I wondered if John and Julia were struggling at school. Julia was going to a big public high school in Maryland, and I was hoping there was a good reason for her to be there, like spending more time with her father. I had gone to Amsterdam several times to see John. He was sharing a puny apartment with his German girlfriend far from the city center and university. His girlfriend insisted they split the rent. Her entire college budget was two thousand euros a year.

"In Germany, I'd be spending six hundred euros a year on college," she pointed out. I found that remarkable, thinking how much US universities charged for tuition. Not only did she speak two languages, but her English proficiency was as good as ours. And I wouldn't have wanted to go up against her in a math contest. You could have said the same thing about most of the young people in Amsterdam too.

Besides the kids and Michael's business, I was stressed over the fact that I was living in Italy as a tourist. I was no longer living in Hoboken, but I was not technically living in Italy either. I was in between. It was unsettling. Though I knew this was largely our fault since we had rushed our move to come before school started in August, we were also people who have the habit of winging it.

So we were stuck in the middle. Neither here nor there. It was like something was purposely slowing us down. Was the world just echoing back to us our worst fears? Or was it Italy being slow?

We were in the land where time-wasting was a national pastime. Italians took long lunches and long vacations. They were loquacious. What the average English speaker says in two sentences, Italians will say in five. I read that Italians lose two weeks a year by standing in line at bureaucratic offices, and that's for a normal year. Never mind if there's any out-of-the-ordinary event going on, like a wedding, birth, funeral, or home purchase. This doesn't include the time it requires to gather documents, get papers stamped, and fill out forms and requests. On top of that, everything required you to *go there*. To pay the condo fees, we had to physically go to the management office so they could run the card through the machine. To pay the electric bill, we had to go to the office of the electric company. To pay our phone bill or put money on our SIM card, we couldn't do it by phone. I mean, don't be ridiculous.

It reminded me of a joke my mother once told me about a poor laborer who had to stand in line every day for everything he did. He had to stand in line for his morning water so he could cook, he had to stand in line to wait for a bus to take him to work, he had to stand in line to collect his pay, and so on. Finally, he was in such despair, he grabbed a machete and went to the palace to kill the king. When he reached the palace, he found a lot of other people, also with machetes, and he was told he would have to stand in line.

My American friend Piera, who studied Chinese medicine, was always talking about mercury retrograde. That's when the planets in our solar system, viewed from Earth, *appear* to pause and go backward. Thus, the word *retrograde*, which comes from the Latin *retrogradus* and means "backward step." This optical illusion happens three or four times a year for three weeks at a time. That's a lot of weeks, and since the planets and stars influence what happens on Earth, astrologers say, it's a time to contemplate and reflect. It is not a time to start new projects, do important business deals, travel, have difficult conversations, or make important decisions, Piera said. And the fact that we were in Italy meant everything would take twice as long anyway, and now I had to worry about mercury retrograde?

Whatever the case, I couldn't stay living in Italy on a tourist visa, even if Italian immigration *were* sleepy.

It was critical that Michael obtain his EU Blue Card too, or work permit, otherwise he wouldn't be able to work and earn money in Italy. He had to do several things to get this done. One task was to get a translated, certified *apostille* copy of all his school transcripts and degrees. This included his high school diploma, college undergraduate diploma, and his master's degree. This was no simple task for someone like Michael. He graduated from high school in Tel Aviv. He graduated from college in New York City, and he received his graduate degree in London.

To get these documents certified, they had to be notarized by the Italian consulate in each city he graduated in. Therefore, he was required to contact three separate Italian consulates in three different countries. For his graduate degree, he contacted his old university in London and asked them to send an official transcript directly to the Italian consulate. Weeks went by, and Michael didn't know what to do since the consulate made it clear that you were not allowed to call or email them. Their motto was "Don't contact us. We'll contact you. Maybe."

Their website stated that if there was a problem with your submission, they wouldn't tell you! You were expected to sit there patiently and wonder what happened to those transcripts as you aged and eventually died. The envelope would arrive, finally, on the day of your funeral. You were supposed to trust the system that hadn't recognized that maybe there was a more efficient way of doing things. It's remarkable how one can be reduced to a state of powerlessness, and it almost makes you wonder if this was by design—a way to remind you that you are a lowly person who needs to pipe down and be obedient and not get any grand ideas that you are important in any way whatsoever.

However, the consulate hadn't considered that there were people like Michael out there in the world. He ignored the *Don't Contact Us Rule* and called every number at the consulate in London until someone answered the phone. It was the housing and local services department. He was informed that the person who handled the job of stamping transcripts in the visa office had retired. The new person hadn't started working there yet.

"When will the new person start then?" Michael asked, hardly believing that his life was held in the balance over having his college transcripts stamped. The person on the line didn't know but told him that the office was six months backlogged, and it could take up to a year to get the certification he needed. Michael didn't have a year. Who does? Luckily, he had a personal contact in the Italian Embassy in Tel Aviv, and he asked that person to please call the London consulate to tell them to get a move on it. In other words, push his application to the front of the line and stamp it—before we are all dead and buried. Miraculously, that worked.

But alas, there was more to the process. Much, much more. Michael was required to get the work visa stamped into his passport at the Italian consulate in New York City. He had to physically take it there. So, he flew to New York and trudged to the consulate, which was in a stinky basement in a building with locked doors and buzzers. The only action required was to stamp his passport, but they couldn't do it on the spot. They didn't have that high level of sophisticated technology yet. Michael was told to leave his passport and come back a few days later, with instructions *not* to contact them.

Meanwhile, I was in Modena. Leopoldo, our dog walker, would come over to walk Domo.

"Mike is in New York?" Leopoldo asked me. I told him yes. He shook his head, as if we had been abandoned. "Poor Jeni and little Domo. All alone."

"It's fine. Honest," I said. "Besides, I need some time alone to work on my book."

Leopoldo frowned. He didn't believe I was fine. "All alone, you and little Domo," he insisted, clucking his tongue.

"I'm fine," I said. "I mean . . . we're fine."

He exhaled. "Call me if you need anything. Okay, honey?"

"Promise."

Leopoldo was so kind and generous. He often brought me gifts: a bonsai tree, Christmas figurine, belt, winter scarf, and bag. He took me to festivals and outlet stores that sold designer clothes. He even showed me how to get a library card.

After Michael got his stamp at the Italian consulate in New York City, cursing his parents and grandparents for not becoming Italian citizens when they had the chance, he flew back to Italy, only to be sent to another immigration office. There, he was hoping this was the end of the process. But no, it was only the beginning. This office gave him a stack of papers to fill out, where he had to provide a multitude of information, such as details about his living abode, including what kind of gas pipes it had, the square footage, and if there was a broom closet. We wanted to write on the form, *We have no broom closet since our home was designed by Numero Uno and his ex-model wife. They aren't aware that us mortals have such things as broom closets.*

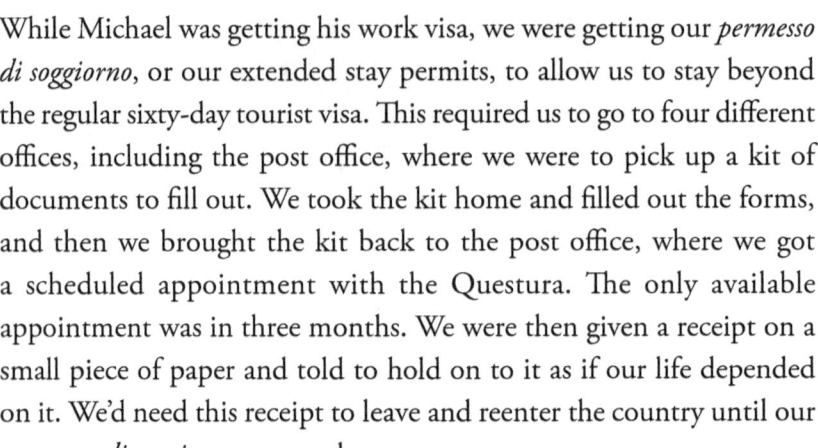

While Michael was getting his work visa, we were getting our *permesso di soggiorno,* or our extended stay permits, to allow us to stay beyond the regular sixty-day tourist visa. This required us to go to four different offices, including the post office, where we were to pick up a kit of documents to fill out. We took the kit home and filled out the forms, and then we brought the kit back to the post office, where we got a scheduled appointment with the Questura. The only available appointment was in three months. We were then given a receipt on a small piece of paper and told to hold on to it as if our life depended on it. We'd need this receipt to leave and reenter the country until our *permesso di soggiorno* was ready.

When we were living in Hoboken and envisioning our romantic life in Italy, I didn't think it would be so complicated. I was under the impression that we could skirt most of the bureaucratic headaches. I'm not sure why I thought that. I suppose it was because of the movie *Under the Tuscan Sun,* where the protagonist moves to Tuscany and buys a villa. She rebuilds her life after her divorce and restores her new home. The movie made perfect sense to me since I had once been a foreign service brat and, in my previous marriage, an international corporate wife when the inconveniences of getting visas were taken care of for us. For all the years I had lived abroad, I realized I had been sheltered from the local bureaucratic offices.

This caused me to ask, *Had I ever fully integrated into the culture of any of the places we lived?* We hung out with mostly expats. When I was a kid, I went to international schools. Later, my kids did too. We were protected and looked after by the embassy or the corporation my ex-husband worked for. We experienced aspects of the cultures we were in and met and befriended locals, and some experiences and encounters were wonderful and life-changing, but we were observers, and we could always leave, or so we assumed.

After three months, we went to our appointments at the Questura, where we each had to bring a photograph of ourselves and be fingerprinted. A month and a half after that, we received a text message with a date to pick up our *permesso di soggiorno* cards at the same location.

In the Questura, we were in an unventilated room that reeked of body odor and was full of people with vacant, bored expressions. Most of them were Nigerians and Somalis, and I thought of the immigrants around Modena and how many were African, forced to sell drugs in the parks or beg on the street for money, like ghosts propped up on street corners. We were told they lived in squalid conditions, and the ones who managed to find apartments were often mistreated by their landlords.

I had once spoken at length with a Nigerian immigrant in Modena who was begging for money. He told me that when he left Nigeria, he'd first gone to Libya and then escaped into Europe by boat. He said he now wanted to go to France. He didn't want to stay in Italy; there was a lack of support for people like him, and he couldn't find work. I listened sympathetically and told him that I had lived in Lagos as a child. He smiled, and we nodded as if that fact made me understand his plight. But the truth was this: my parents and I lived on Ikoyi Island, which was a plush residential neighborhood with manicured lawns and big houses. Our house was gated and spacious, and we had a staff of five. My parents were Master and Madam, according to local custom. I didn't exactly know the same Nigeria he did.

Matteo Salvini was on the rise at the time, the far-right interior minister nicknamed *Il Capitano,* responsible for Italy's policing, national security, and immigration policies. He was called anti-migrant, Eurosceptic, and a right-wing populist leader. He was referred to as "the most feared man in Europe" and had "jolted Europe's establishment." He had been ominously featured on the cover of *Time Magazine*, with a close-up of his face in black-and-white as he smiled cunningly. The magazine claimed he was "the new face of Europe" and on "a mission to undo the EU." He held rallies dressed in jeans and green sneakers, with a beer in his hand, and spoke of putting Italians first and seizing back control of the EU's faceless bureaucrats. Immigration was a controversial issue after the collapse of Syria, which had triggered the biggest exodus since WWII. Salvini stated that there weren't enough jobs for Italians, and now the state would be forced to take care of hordes of migrants from across the Mediterranean. He pointed out that many immigrants entered Italy illegally, not because they had relations there or good prospects but because it was easier to reach than other EU countries. Under EU law, migrants were obliged to settle in the first EU country in which they landed, and Italy was the closest point in Europe to the migrant smuggling centers in Libya. Salvini had made a pledge to deport 500,000 undocumented immigrants from Italy and to suspend asylum procedures until the EU agreed to a fair distribution of refugees. He was ousted from power the following year but reinstated in 2022.

We saw Marco's friend behind the window. There was a long line of people slowly inching forward in front of him. We waited, but when the officer caught Michael's eye, he shooed away the poor soul he had been helping with the flick of his hand. The man looked confused but stepped back obediently. We gave the man an apologetic glance, feeling awful. It was not only degrading to be flicked away with the motion of the officer's hand, but we were clearly privileged with options. We came to Italy not because we were running away from a war-torn country, horrific living conditions, or human rights abuses but simply because we felt like living in Italy. We didn't want to live in the US at that moment. You know, the country that purported to be the land of opportunity and wealth.

Growing up as a foreign service brat, I was taught to respect other cultures. My classmates were from all over the world, and my parents and I would learn as much as we could about the country we were living in, but the idea of American exceptionalism was branded into my brain. When we lived in Lagos, Manila, and Rangoon, gazed at the poverty, and observed the restricted, fearful lives of the locals, we clucked our tongues. My parents would tell me to be thankful that I was an American. We had freedom. We were the lucky ones in the world.

And perhaps we were because, in the Questura, we were getting pushed up to the front of the line, prioritized.

The immigration officer beckoned for us impatiently, and with apprehension, we approached the glass window. We were pathetically deferential, displaying the colorful and flowery language that Italians loved to hear. "*Buongiorno signore. Grazie mille,*" we said as he looked at us with all seriousness, pretending we hadn't jumped the line 'cause we were buddies with his buddy. No. This was a very serious matter indeed. There were "procedures" to follow (wink, wink, nod, nod). We smiled broadly and told Marco's friend we were impressed with his country and would like our *"permesso di soggiorno, per favore."* We gave him our papers.

As the officer inspected our passports and papers, I thought about why I was doing this, wondering if I had succumbed to romantic delusion. Italy was referred to as "the sick man in Europe." It was the only EU member in a recession. Italy had a debt-laden economy, an aging population, and a high unemployment rate, and young Italians were forced to find jobs in other EU countries or continue to live with their parents. And the country was suffering from years of government ineptitude and corruption. It was the birthplace of Fascism. Would that ideology return?

Although, when it came to the US, and despite the fact that I had been indoctrinated with the idea of American exceptionalism, I could now see that the American system was not as exceptional as I had been led to believe. It's health-care, education, and political systems, often times, worked against the common man. And let's not forget industrialized farming, corporatocracy, the class war, poverty, a crumbling infrastructure, corporate media, wastefulness and excess, the military-industrial complex, and its war machine. Did I leave anything out? Perhaps we should have had a Michelin Guide for Best Country in the World, based on a strict criterion of what constitutes *the best.*

So, maybe the whole world was broken, in various degrees. However, Michael and I were not interested in Italian residency because of their economy. We, like almost all starstruck Americans who dreamed of living in Italy, were drawn to the culture, food, language, beaches, and landscape—the Tuscan villa fantasy. In our privileged, spoiled minds, this Italian dream was an escape from all the rotten systems of the world. But was there such a thing as an escape, even for us? Here in the Questura, where we were surrounded by those who had fled from something dangerous, was it possible that we were deluding ourselves into thinking that we could simply step out of the loop?

The immigration officer finally handed us our *permesso di soggiorno*. It had been five months since the process started, and the date on the card was from the date we requested it, so in the year the visa was valid, five months had already been used up. Then the process would start again. This included getting a new photo and getting re-fingerprinted. But we'd worry about it again in . . . seven months.

When we were dismissed, we profusely thanked Marco's friend and then high-tailed it out of the building, leaving the poor zombie-looking migrants behind, feeling a tug at our hearts that most of them didn't have options like we did. With our eyes blinking from the bright sun, we breathed in the Italian air, feeling proud of ourselves. We were experiencing the real Italy, not just the fantasy. We were shown some hard realities, but hey, we managed to get through the door. Even with connections, that was saying something.

Chapter Six

When filing for residency, we realized we could cut out bureaucratic steps if we became husband and wife. We wanted to get married for other reasons too, obviously. We loved each other and had been sharing a life together for six years. We told our family and close friends we were getting married but made no formal announcement. We would go to the courthouse, say our vows, and sign the paperwork. We didn't want to make a fuss.

We applied for a marriage license at the Ufficio dell'Anagrafe, where we had to register, fill out paperwork, and get a permit. We were required to go to the US consulate in Florence, about a two-hour train ride, to get our papers stamped. After that, we took the paperwork back to the Ufficio dell'Anagrafe, where a woman behind a glass window told us the stamp on the paper was the wrong stamp. So we went back to the US consulate in Florence to get the right stamp. When all was said and done, we weren't sure we had saved any time after all.

One of the other requirements was a notarized document that stated I was not married to someone else. Michael did not need this document to get married, and I found that infuriating. In Italy, during the Fascist period when Mussolini reigned supreme, women were considered inferior to men and expected to be subservient. The woman's purpose was to have babies, to populate the country with good little fascists. Since then, there had been advancement in equality for women, but it was still a very patriarchal society.

I read that Italians typically get married later than Americans, and their divorce rate is low compared to other EU countries. I could only imagine the paperwork involved when someone wanted to get a divorce. The hoops they'd have to jump through and the bureaucratic offices they'd have to endure would surely discourage anyone from going through with it. Italian couples also tend to have only one child. Italy has the lowest birth rate in the European Union and one of the lowest in the world.

"What does this entail?" I asked Michael, wondering if the government officials enjoyed finding ways to fill our days with busywork.

"We need to have four Italian witnesses who are willing to swear to the fact that you're not leading a double life," Michael said, smirking.

"Four witnesses? Not five? Or three?"

"No. Four."

"I see," I said. "So, you can be a bigamist, but I can't. Is that what you're saying?" Michael could be married in ten other countries, but nobody cared about that, apparently.

Michael smiled.

We summoned up four of our Italian friends, including the gelato maker, Gianluca. They agreed to go to the notary office to sign a legal document as to the "purity of my soul" or something to that effect. Four friends, who we had just met and only knew about my life in Italy, took my word for it that I was divorced.

The evening of my appointment, we took a taxi to the notary office since we were in between renting cars. I still hadn't gotten my Alfa Romeo. The office was on the edge of town, and Gianluca hitched a ride with us. The three of us sat in the back seat. We cruised out of the historic center and toward the nondescript commercial district that looked industrial and drab. The sky was darkening, and headlights flashed on as we passed office buildings, apartment complexes, and occasional X-rated "sexy shops."

There was a slight tinge of gray in the air. Cities in the north of Italy are rated among the worst in Europe for air pollution since the northern cities are industrial centers, and Modena, which is in a valley where wind levels are low, was at the top of the list.

"Have you ever listened to the Grateful Dead?" Michael asked Gianluca. He was prompting a rather deep discussion for being in a taxi on the way to a notary office. Since Michael was a "Deadhead," he asked everyone who was into classic rock music that question. I never imagined I'd marry a Deadhead. Before I met him, I hadn't known what it meant.

"I'm not too familiar with them," Gianluca said, shaking his head.

"I'll get you listening to them." Michael said. He and I clutched each other's hands, unified. I was willing to take one for the team by going through this moronic exercise at the notary office so we could finally legalize our relationship.

Michael then explained to Gianluca how the Grateful Dead improvised. I remembered reading Amy Tan's memoir called *Where the Past Begins*, where she describes how MRI imagery was done on jazz pianists who improvise in their playing. What they found was that the front lobes of their brains, responsible for being rational and staying under control, were less active. Writers (as Amy Tan explains) can also improvise in their work. When this happens, it allows them to write freely without knowing where the scene is going to take them. Most often, this is when the best writing comes through.

I was half listening to the conversation but increasingly fading the men out. *I'm in Italy, in a taxi, sitting between a Deadhead and a gelato maker, about to sign a paper in an Italian notary office to swear I'm not married so I can get married again.* I kept thinking about the Joan Rivers joke about marriages: "Half of all marriages end in divorce, and then there are the really unhappy ones."

In Hoboken, Michael was often in Israel or Italy, and I would go out with friends alone. I recalled one night, when Michael was away, and I went to a bar with friends: two married couples and two divorced men. The two couples sat on one side of the table, while us divorcées sat on the other side. The divorcée men and I began exchanging horror stories about our divorces, and we discovered that we had each given up our beloved pets to our ex-spouses. We exclaimed how utterly unfair that was, and we jokingly decided to create a divorce support group called "Exes Without Pets." I enjoyed being on the single side of the table that night, with our secret inside jokes.

I hadn't been to a lot of weddings in my life, but I had been to my mother's when she married my stepfather in Jerusalem and my dad's when he married my stepmother in Washington, DC. I was at my grandfather's wedding when he was eighty and married after my grandmother died. I also went to the two weddings my stepfather had after my mom passed away. For me, weddings were the end of an era more than the beginning of something new.

I was nervous about marriage, naturally, because I had gone through a terribly bitter divorce. But my level of commitment to Michael was not in question. He was my best friend. He knew me better than anyone else in the world, and likewise for me of him, and we still loved each other and thought the other amazing. Six years before, we had fallen wildly in love, so much so that we were willing to sacrifice for our love, like it was on an altar for the gods in a holy shrine on a mountain reaching toward the heavens. We changed the direction of our lives to be together, hurting people along the way. Perhaps it was that blind idealism that was making me hesitate. Back then, we had felt invincible, infallible, capable of doing anything we set our minds to. We had been reckless. I thought, *Are we being reckless now?*

I suddenly didn't feel well. My stomach was in knots, and I remembered the lamb chops Michael had prepared for lunch that day. I complained that the meat tasted strange but ate it anyway. As we bumped along, my mere upset stomach turned into nausea. I put my hand on my mouth, and I asked Michael to tell the driver to pull over. We were in rush hour traffic, and in confusion, the driver slowed down, and that detonated a cacophony of blaring horns.

"*Mia moglie sta male!*" Michael shouted. My wife is sick!

The driver immediately careened around a corner, pulled to the side of the road, and screeched to a stop. I clamored over Michael and out of the car just in time to barf all over the grass. I was vomiting out my fear of being alone and abandoned. Fear that this marriage wouldn't last like my last one. If it didn't, what would that say about me? I moved all the time, moved locations, but did that have to include husbands too?

I was partially aware that the taxi had left, and Gianluca, who had disappeared for a short time, suddenly materialized with a bottle of water. I took it gratefully and gulped it down before we proceeded to walk toward the notary building in the dark, headlights from oncoming traffic glaring in our eyes. Then we saw our destination, like a lighted hostel in a midnight storm. The fact that they had a bathroom was all I cared about. The nausea had not left me. Once we got to the building, Michael and I stood outside the entrance while Gianluca went inside.

"Nervous about the prospect of getting married again?" Michael asked. I told him once about how my ex-husband had been sick the day before our wedding. My mom and I had to rush him to a health clinic late at night. His blood pressure was so high, the doctor accused him of being a heroin addict. I wondered if Michael was thinking about that.

"No," I said defensively.

"Are you sure?"

"Yes," I insisted. His questioning was making me angry, like it was accusatory. But it wasn't that at all; he could sense my fear. He knew me so well.

"If you don't want to," he said, "we don't have to. I mean, I've always thought of us as married anyway. You're my soulmate. I don't need a piece of paper to tell me that."

If I had any doubts before, then this certainly helped squash them. If I reached underneath my fear of marriage, really examining it, I'd see that it had nothing to do with what marriage required. I loved the idea of being committed to that one special person for life. And maybe this time, after being together for so many years, after moving to Italy, we were acting like adults about this and doing something... sensible? "I want to get married," I said. "But do *you* want to get married?"

Michael looked at me directly. "Yes, Jennifer." He sighed. "I've known since the moment we fell in love that we would spend the rest of our lives together."

Inside, as I stood in the notary office, in my puke-splattered shoes, the exchange was in Italian, but I imagined the notary said to our friends, *Do you swear that this woman is not married to another man somewhere else in the world? That she is single, honest, and true?*

Our friends: *We do, Signore.*

Our friends signed the document stating this fact, and then I signed it, to swear my friends were not liars. Michael paid the man three hundred euros, and we all left the building. We could now collectively breathe a sigh of relief that I was not a bigamist. I was sure the papers would be filed away in some drawer—the infamous drawer where all useless papers go—and would never see the light of day again.

Soon after we got home, Michael got violently ill. That solved it. We had food poisoning. I was not just having pre-wedding jitters after all.

While we were planning our wedding, we moved to another apartment. It was just outside the historic center on Via Nicola Fabrizi, considered one of the best residential streets in town. Our apartment was in a 1970s-style building across the street from a park with tall trees and a walking path.

It was a large two-bedroom, two-bathroom apartment on the second floor that had been renovated, so it was new and fresh. It had high ceilings, lots of windows, and marble and hardwood floors. The front door opened into an entrance hall, and around the corner was an enormous living room and an office with a built-in bookcase. The kitchen was smaller than the last one but more modern and functional (though we had no microwave—we didn't in the other place either—

and it was remarkable how much we didn't miss it). Off the kitchen was a laundry room. It used to function as the maid's room with its own private entrance.

Our new landlord was amicable and accommodating. Before moving in, he put screens on the windows and installed central air-conditioning (upon our insistence). Before that, the windows were kept open in the summer heat, which allowed hordes of mosquitoes to invade. The new apartment was not furnished, so we sent for our things in Hoboken.

When our shipment arrived, we hung our art on the walls, put our Oriental rugs on the floors, placed our furniture in the rooms, and put my books on the shelves. So many of them about travel: *Burmese Days* by George Orwell, *A Passage to India* by E.M. Forster, *Travels with My Aunt* by Graham Greene, and *Lost Horizon* by James Hilton, books my mother had given to me throughout the years, relics of my past.

We had given away our sofa in Hoboken, so we needed to purchase a new one. But since we didn't have a sofa in our living room yet, someone suggested we use that space to hire a band for our wedding reception. We remembered a klezmer band we had listened to on a street corner one day in Modena called *Swingari*. There were four young musicians, none of them Jewish, even though klezmer music is traditional folk music of the Ashkenazi Jews. It's fast and haunting and sounds like laughter. We had their CD and found the lead band member's card, a clarinet player named Vincenzo. Michael called him and hired the band for our wedding.

Our simple idea of having a small gathering of friends after our wedding ceremony turned into a wedding reception with a band and catered food. Michael's sister, DeeDee, from New York, flew in to attend our celebration. Marco volunteered to provide the wine and champagne, and Gianluca said he'd make the dessert. If anything, we conceded, it was an excuse to get all our friends from Italy together.

We had a quiet civil ceremony at the municipality, the Palazzo Communale, in the Piazza Grande, where, ominously, executions were once performed. It was February, and there was a misty cold rain, and everything looked gray and depressing, but our moods were bright.

It turned out not to be such a casual affair. Michael wore a suit, and I wore a blue dress that he helped pick out. Our ceremony was presided over by an official, wearing a large yellow sash over a suit, who officiated in Italian as we sat in an ornate room with a high ceiling and old portraits on the walls. After each statement, all we had to say was, "*sì*," and then we signed the marriage certificate. Our friends, Abbie and Andrea, were our witnesses, while DeeDee took pictures. Michael and I were married.

After the wedding ceremony, we had lunch at Carlo Alberto's La Lumira with Abbie, Andrea, and DeeDee and then our reception/cocktail party in the evening at our apartment for all our friends, which turned into an Italian-Jewish hybrid wedding bash. It was funny considering all the guests, except for DeeDee, were Catholic. The guest list included the usual fair and some of our newfound Italian friends, movers, and shakers of Modena, including Lara. As our band played klezmer, our Italian friends were dressed to the nines and arrived with gifts and flowers. We schmoozed and laughed and drank too much and caught whiffs of the band's marijuana smoke during their breaks on our patio. Leopoldo was sloshing back the wine while Wayne shot him admiring glances. Beppe was opening more bottles of champagne—Marco brought enough to supply a small village—DeeDee took charge of taking photographs and made everyone smile into the camera, and Gianluca hung out in the kitchen, arranging his homemade chocolates and pralines on a tray. Abbie and Andrea and Enrico and Courtney made their rounds as honorary hosts, and I flitted around the room in a blur, acutely aware that I was on display, the bride, and I never liked being the center of attention. But it was a lovely evening, and I was having a terrific time, giddy that I was married again, to my soulmate this time.

When the party was in full swing, DeeDee, who had made herself the master of Jewish ceremonies, instructed some of us to form a circle, and we joined hands and danced the hora, while the other guests clapped along. I had never seen Michael dance before, but he was having fun, even though this was not at all what we had originally planned, and this whole thing had gone in an entirely different direction. But when did anything go as planned?

Later, DeeDee grabbed a chair, sat me down, and instructed some of the men to lift me. She wanted us to do the hora dance where the bride and groom are lifted on chairs as the guests dance around them. The Catholic men looked at her, bewildered, but obliged. "Higher!" DeeDee shouted above the music. They lifted me a foot more, giving each other looks and shrugs. "Higher!" DeeDee shouted again. They didn't get it, and finally everyone gave up.

Chapter Seven

A couple of weeks after our wedding, Beppe suggested we come to Palermo. He and Antonella had their main residence in Modena, but they had an apartment in Palermo. He was trying to convince Michael to find investors for the soccer team Palermitana. Michael was considering it since things were not going well with the old-age home business project.

Beppe volunteered to pick us up at the airport, and soon after we landed and collected our luggage, we spotted him standing at the entrance with the bright Sicilian sunlight reflecting behind him and his hands on his hips, looking like a Marvel superhero. When he saw us, he shouted, "Mr. Mike, Ah-Jeni!" Then swaggered toward us with his arms outstretched, prepared to give us hugs and kisses. I was excited to be in Sicily, and who better to show us around than Beppe, the man who was born and raised in Palermo?

I read that Sicily is the size of Norway and the biggest island in the Mediterranean. I also read that it had been conquered by the Greeks, then the Byzantines, then the Muslims, then the Normans, then the Bourbons (the French), and then the Spanish. I was impressed that Palermo, a seaside city, was once a wealthy and majestic center. We could still see evidence of this from its royal palace, cathedrals, and famous opera house. It felt grounded, proud of its diverse mix of cultures and its ability to adapt. It was proof that humanity endures and survives, warning us not to get too attached to a particular way of life. There might be something else around the corner.

The one thing that was certain in Italy was the rivalry between the North and the South. If you look at a map of Italy, there is an invisible line called *il mezzogiorno*, which signifies a clear division between the North and South. Northerners call Southerners *terroni*, from the root word for earth (terra). It's the equivalent of calling someone a hick. Southerners call Northerners *polentoni*, which means "polenta eaters." On the face of it, that didn't sound like much of an insult, except Northerners eat a lot of polenta dishes, and it's considered a drudge food.

Before Italy was united 150 years ago, the North and South were divided culturally and economically. While the South was conquered by invaders, the North was conquered by the Nordic Germanic tribes and ruled by Austria for centuries. This resulted in an identity crisis for Italy. But for Beppe, it meant he was caught between two worlds. Between life and death, as he had put it.

"Do you know Frank Sinatra?" Beppe asked in the airport parking lot. We were walking to his car, and he was chivalrously pulling my suitcase.

"Yes," I said. "Who hasn't?" I didn't bother to mention that Ol' Blue Eyes was the most famous native son of Hoboken.

Beppe stopped, looked at me, and said beamingly, "He's from Sicily!" He then continued walking, and we followed. But after a few seconds, he said, "Do you know John Travolta?"

"Yes, I've heard of him too," I said with a slight chuckle.

"He's from Sicily!" Beppe proclaimed.

"No kidding," I said politely. I enjoyed this game. It made our walk more interesting.

"Do you know Lady Gaga?"

"Let me guess—"

"She is from Sicily!" Beppe said with such happiness that I wanted to believe it with all my heart too. With enough time to kill, he would eventually tell me that all Italian culture and language was born in Sicily, while, really, the modern Italian language was born in Tuscany.

For the next few days, Beppe took us around his beloved city, to the many sites in Palermo. He also had us try famous Sicilian dishes such as: linguine al limone, pasta alla norma, granita, cassata, and cannoli. And, of course, Palermo's street foods such as arancine (rice balls), panelle (chickpea fritters), and pani ca' meusa, or "spleen sandwich," which is a combination of veal spleen, lung, and cartilage from a calf's throat. I ate it all while Beppe watched, amused. He didn't know who he was dealing with. I had been eating all kinds of weirdnesses since I was barely out of diapers, living in the exotic places that I had.

One night, Beppe took us to his apartment, where Antonella was preparing dinner for us. Their dog, a bug-eyed Chihuahua, was running in circles, thrilled to have company. He jumped up on my legs and let out a yap.

"Gucci! Leave Jeni alone!" Antonella scolded, shaking a finger at him. Gucci quieted down, though not before he let out a muffled bark and scampered away. But he was soon back with a small, stuffed teddy bear. He dropped it at my feet, a clear invitation that he wanted us to play a game. I threw the toy, and he took off running. This repeated time and again.

The living room had heavy furniture, a large TV, and framed pictures of the family on a console, including photographs of their two daughters (one being our vet) and Beppe and Antonella in their younger years, looking gorgeous. They were a chronology of the family's best years, proudly displayed, and I happily lingered over them before following Antonella into the kitchen. The men had wandered off, and we assumed they were talking about business or soccer.

As Antonella chopped vegetables, she told me that her grandmother had castrated the roosters for everyone in her village. "My grandmother cut off the balls," she said, as if the method of castration needed explaining to me. "She was very good at it," she added proudly.

I chuckled over the fact that this was even a thing, but being a rooster castrator was an important job. Italians make broth with castrated roosters. The Italian word for these unfortunate roosters is *capone*. An intact rooster is called a *galletto*. This pointed out the level of detail that Italians consider when cooking a dish. *No, we cannot use a galletto or even a plain old chicken. We must use the capone to make broth!*

Gucci yapped when I forgot to throw his teddy bear. He gave up after a minute, pranced to a table, sat on his haunches, and barked. He was looking up at a worn-looking pillow.

"No, Gucci," Antonella said harshly. "You can't have that now!" He tilted his head.

"What does he want?" I asked.

"He likes to make love to the pillow," Antonella said candidly. I nodded as I tried not to laugh. Gucci shamelessly scampered back to me and put his paw on my foot. Since he couldn't hump his pillow, he wanted to continue our game. I threw his teddy, and off he went.

The summer before, I had also vacationed in Sicily. I took John and Julia to the small seaside town of San Vito Lo Capo. It was about an hour outside of Palermo. Antonella had encouraged me to vacation there and helped me find a place to rent for two weeks.

It was meant to be a respite, a chance for John, Julia, and I to spend quality time together before spending the rest of the summer in Modena, where Michael was with his three daughters who were visiting from Tel Aviv. All five kids wanted to spend time together too. Plus, Julia got a summer internship working for Food for Soul, a nonprofit in Modena started by Massimo Bottura and Lara to deal with food waste and redefine community kitchens. Lara was kind enough to put Julia in contact with the staff of Food for Soul, where she had submitted her resumé.

When the time came, we flew to Palermo from Bologna. John had flown in from Amsterdam, and Julia from the States. I had texted

Antonella our arrival details, and she arranged a driver for us. She told me his name was Benedetto. He'd drive us to our apartment in San Vito Lo Capo, and she'd meet us there and introduce me to the landlady.

As soon as the kids and I walked into the main terminal building in Palermo, laden with our luggage, I spotted Benedetto. He was a heavyset Sicilian man with a big sign around his neck that read, *JENNY*. We nodded a greeting, he took our luggage, and we followed him to the parking lot. Then we stopped in front of a small, broken-down hatchback. Antonella had said he would pick us up in a big new van, so I was surprised the car was so . . . dinky. I gave him an alarmed look, and he threw up his arms and ranted in Italian as he shoved one of our large suitcases in the car. I guessed he was explaining that something happened to the van and this small hatchback was all he could come up with instead. I hesitated, but there was nothing we could do. San Vito Lo Capo was more than an hour drive away.

"This car doesn't have a trunk," I said. Benedetto ignored me. He didn't understand a word of English. I said a few words in Italian, but he ignored that too. I figured I was mangling the language. It reminded me of *Murder by Death*, when the blind butler and the mute cook were trying to communicate with each other.

Benedetto grabbed the other suitcases. He rolled them to the front passenger side, tried to open the door, but it was stuck. "*Ma vaffanculo!*" he cursed, throwing up his arms. He pulled the suitcases to the other side, opened the driver's door, and crammed the remaining two pieces of luggage inside until they were perched onto the front passenger's seat, which left only the snug back seat for the three of us. We climbed in and sat shoulder to shoulder, where there were no seat belts. Benedetto squeezed in behind the wheel, turned the engine, and gunned out of the lot and onto the main road, where he swerved in and out of cars and perilously turned corners.

"*Scusi*," I said, grabbing the seat and looking on my phone for the best way to say "slow down" in Italian. When I found it, I shouted, "*Troppo veloce!*"

We zipped along curvy mountain roads in the dark with reckless zest while the kids and I held on and prayed we wouldn't be the victims of a five-car pileup somewhere up ahead. The road emptied as we neared the coast. This only encouraged Benedetto to drive faster. Then his cell phone rang, and he picked it up without a care in the world. He had one hand on the wheel.

"Ciao," he said cheerfully. "Si. Carlo!"

"*No telefono!*" I shouted, imagining these to be my last words on this earth.

We miraculously arrived in San Vito Lo Capo alive. Benedetto stopped in front of a small complex in the center of the village near the beach. I rolled down the window and poked my head out, trying to spot Antonella in the darkness. I saw her, or the silhouette of her, standing next to another woman, who I soon learned was the landlady named Enza. We got out of the car, struggled to pull our suitcases out, and followed Antonella and Enza into the building.

The two-bedroom apartment was sparse. It had a tile floor and furniture that looked like it belonged to someone's grandmother. It had a patio to hang-dry the laundry, plus a rooftop balcony with a view of the town and sea. The balcony was too hot to sit during the day, and the umbrella on the table wouldn't be useful since we couldn't open it due to the wind.

There was no internet, much to the kids' dismay, and only one wall air conditioner in the hallway, which meant none of the bedrooms got air. I suppose I should have been thankful that there was that, at least. I heard mosquitoes buzzing and concluded I'd have to shut the windows.

We had neighbors who were also tourists—there were beach towels hanging from their balcony rail—but we were the only foreigners. In our two weeks there, none of the neighbors attempted to speak to us. The only people we knew were Beppe and Antonella.

The next morning, while the kids slept, I walked to the beach. I soaked in the quiet sound of the waves, took a deep breath of the salty air, and held it in my lungs as the water rolled over my bare feet. Sand, rocks, and bits of shell gently poked at my skin as my feet sank farther into the sand beneath the water. I was comforted by the feeling of the earth, the grounded-ness of it. I was thankful for the gorgeous water, translucent as a swimming pool. I loved it. It made sense since I am a water sign: sensitive, imaginative, impulsive, and intuitive. I felt at peace, liberated.

I plunged in and got stung by a jellyfish. An enormous, burning blister formed on my arm. I went to the pharmacy for cream, then navigated to a grocery store to buy lunch and essentials. Julia called and said, "While you're at the store, Mom, could you please pick me up makeup wipes, wax strips, and an electric fan?" as if I was popping over to Walmart instead of a dinky grocery store in a remote Sicilian village more than an hour from pockets of civilization.

San Vito Lo Capo was beautiful, quaint, exactly the sort of place I wanted to be. It was a small provincial beach town on the Tyrrhenian Sea with turquoise Caribbean-like water. It had white block houses, apartments on narrow streets with palm trees, and plump Italian grandmothers sitting outside. Monte Monaco loomed above and shone pink in the evenings against the setting sun.

I wanted this to be a special vacation for us and for everything to go perfectly. I'd get up early to rent lounge chairs and umbrellas and reserve a spot by the sea, and then I'd get snacks and bottled water and make sandwiches for later. I'd lug the towels, snorkels, books, and food to my reserved spot on the beach. I'd swim with the kids, clean, do laundry, trek to the grocery store and pharmacy. The pharmacist began to recognize me, the American who struggled to speak Italian but always had some ailment to treat, a jellyfish sting, sunburn, menstrual cramps, headaches, or cuts. The kids helped me cook and do laundry, but I had a deep maternal need to nurture. Empty nest syndrome, I supposed. And guilt that we were all scattered around the world had something to do with it too.

On the beach, I lathered myself up with 50 SPF sunscreen and sat under an umbrella, while the Italian women laid out directly in the sun, deeply tanned already, chain-smoking cigarettes. The younger women changed their bathing suits several times a day. Even at the beach, it was a fashion show. One Italian woman I met in Modena told me she took no less than ten bathing suits with her on beach vacations and changed at least three times a day.

I watched the beachgoers, read my book, or sat and stared at the water and took in the cacophony of summer beach sounds. I loved that we were vacationing with the locals, and we seemed to be the only Americans around. There were no information or welcome centers with pamphlets of things to do and see. No maps to show us where to go. It was perfect.

I connected more with the South of Italy than the North. I found it unpretentious and authentic. Like Beppe said once, "In the North they live in a dream, in the South, the reality." For me, the South *was* the Italian dream, the one I had pictured in my mind when I was in New York. Traditional, with close-knit families, relaxed, amazing seafood, and sun. There was no pretending that they were not corrupted, that their architectural treasures had crumbled. Their pain and blemishes were out for everyone to plainly see.

One afternoon, we went on a boat tour to the Lo Zingaro Nature Reserve and boarded a small boat with about ten Italian tourists. The skipper and his first mates, two young, tanned men, set off on the calm sea on that warm, sunny, picture-perfect day. Everyone was all smiles as we sailed past coves and grottoes in the limestone cliffs along the coast. On one side of us was nothing but endless sea, and on the other side were sandy beaches and rock formations that jutted out of the water. Throughout the day, the boat stopped in several locations and anchored; then the skipper encouraged us to get in the water. We needed no encouragement, and we put on our masks and snorkels and jumped in the warm turquoise sea. The kids and I laughed and dove deep, looking at the fish, and then we popped our heads out to gaze at the amazing scenery. We were in gleeful disbelief that we were in the Mediterranean Sea in Sicily.

At the end of the day, when we were sailing back to San Vito Lo Capo, feeling tired but content, the wind picked up. Then the water got choppy. The skipper took a firm grip on the wheel while the first mate kept a lookout. Soon, the boat ascended a wave. It dawned on me that none of us were wearing life vests. In that instant, we took flight into the blue yonder, and for a moment, we free-fell until we crashed down into a thunderous splash, white-knuckled, clenching the sides of the boat. Everyone shrieked and screamed, gurgling as torrents of water splashed our faces. When we finally arrived at the pier in San Vito Lo Capo, thoroughly drenched and shaken, one passenger, who could speak a little English, said, "The name of this boat means God's Shower!" We climbed out of the boat, our senses out of whack and our spines out of alignment.

One morning, we woke up early and set off to climb Monte Monaco, the mountain that loomed over the town. The early morning air was cool and refreshing. There were farms, and the road toward the mountain was quiet. Yet we noticed there were no signs to direct us, and we had a difficult time finding the path that would take us up the mountain, a path that had once been an old donkey trail. We stopped and asked people where the trail was, but nobody seemed to know, so we continued. Our only option was to randomly pick a direction and walk, or go back, and we didn't want to do that.

More than an hour later, we finally found the path that led up the mountain. And wouldn't you know, there *were* signs to direct tourists to the mountain trail, but they had fallen, battered and broken, half buried in the dirt. As we stared at the busted-up signs, I reminded myself that this was Sicily, it didn't operate so neatly, and that was part of its charm.

The path up the mountain was narrow, with stones and thorny vegetation, and by the time we began clambering up, we had lost the cooler morning air. A couple of fit hikers carrying large canteens of water briskly passed us and disappeared into the distance. I was drenched with sweat and stared at our meager water supply. I could feel the burn in my legs and chest, but the scenery was alluring, and each turn promised another view of lush plains against the blue sea; the air smelled of salt and pasture. There was a serenity to the island. The problems of our lives and living in Modena temporarily evaporated. I thought of how close we were to the North African coast. This is what I loved about our world: there were still spots that felt secluded and exotic. It felt good to be alone, together, in the quiet wind. After a while, John and Julia were walking ahead as I swatted a few flies away from my face. We didn't know how much longer we had, and we felt we had already been walking on this trail for hours (but probably only thirty minutes). I was astonished at my gasps and labored breathing, and the kids looked concerned.

"Are you okay, Mom?" Julia asked.

"I'm fine," I said. "I'm just hot and tired."

"This is supposed to be an easy trail, Mom," John said. "I mean, if donkeys can do it—"

"I'm out of shape," I said, trying not to lose my footing on the rocky pathway. Or *Perhaps I am exhausted from lack of sleep? From cooking? Cleaning? Swimming? Trips to the pharmacy?* "And we didn't bring enough water," I added. I plopped down on a rock. "You go on ahead without me," I said as if I was an injured soldier in battle and I had no will left to live. Both John and Julia shook their heads. The pity they felt was palpable. Already I had sped through Sicilian mountain roads, swam in jellyfish-infested waters, rode through ocean swells, and tried to scale a mountain without enough water in the sweltering heat. I needed to chill out.

We stopped to rest, listening to the buzz of insects and the sound of the rolling sea.

"Uh . . . Mom," John said after a moment. "There's a cow."

Julia giggled. I turned and looked behind me, and sure enough, there was a cow. We let her majesty, in her doleful manner, meander past us, and we watched her clop away.

"Where did she come from?" Julia asked.

"From one of the farms around here, I suppose," I said.

"Talk about free-range!" John said, and we all laughed.

I looked at the farmland and flat, verdant pastures below us. It seemed

San Vito Lo Capo was as agreeable a seaside town as one could find, the perfect little Italian tourist spot. I felt a rush of gratitude to be there and to be with my children. We were where we were supposed to be.

In Palermo with Beppe, Antonella, and Michael, we strolled up and down Corso Vittorio Emanule and Via Maqueda that intersects at Quattro Canti. We went to the Capo Street market, Piazza Bellini, and Piazza Pretoria. There wasn't a piazza we didn't see. We went to the Palermo Cathedral, the Church of the Gesù, and the Church of San Cataldo.

Beppe cheerfully pointed out the "No Mafia" signs that were scattered around the city, bullet holes in buildings from WWII, and the Fascist Period architecture that was easily recognizable with their imposing, monolithic block shapes. All the while, Beppe said things like "Modena is shit, but Sicily is perfect." Or "The Modenese are snobs, but the Sicilians are friendly." Or "You know the Boss? Bruce Springsteen? He's from Sicily!"

Beppe took us to a soccer game (Italians call it football). It was the first time I had ever been to a pro-league soccer match. Beppe explained that football (soccer) is one of the bastions of Italian pride. It's like a religion. The soccer fans in Italy are loyal to their favorite team, with a ferocity that is hard-pressed to be seen anywhere else in the world. It's tribal, and it's for life. There's a saying: "You can change your wife, family, and job, but you can't change your soccer club."

The stadium was full of shouting fans, and that night, the Palermitana team won the game, and Beppe beamed. "You see how good they are?" he said to Michael. "They need to get back to Serie A, and they will!"

Michael explained to me that Palermitana had been in Serie A, the premier division in Italian professional football, but dropped to second division, Serie B. Serie A is made up of twenty teams and is regarded as one of the best football leagues in the world. If Palermitana got into the premier division again, they would be attractive to investors since they'd have lucrative TV rights. That alone was worth tens of millions.

On our last night, we went to dinner at a seafood restaurant with Beppe, Antonella, and a woman named Valentina. She worked for the Palermitana Soccer Club and was close to the owner of the team, il Commendatore (a pseudonym, obviously). Michael had told me that the owner was interested in selling the team because the team was suffering financially from all the money that he and his cronies had sucked out of it. Nobody was putting it that way, of course, and it was only a suspicion, but the Palermitana team had suffered through a series of shady owners.

The restaurant glowed brightly as we sat at a table next to a large window that overlooked a pier. Beppe ordered the wines and dominated the conversation while Antonella looked mildly amused. Gucci sat in her purse with his head sticking out. He went everywhere she went.

Valentina asked Michael and me about our trip to Palermo. What did we think of it? We told her we were enjoying the city very much, and we recounted all the places we had seen. Valentina smiled, pleased that we had connected with the city. Beppe smiled too. He had made the introductions. We were all hoping this would lead to something exciting and lucrative.

Chapter Eight

The Italian old-age project had been officially put on hold, but Michael was optimistic about his prospects of making money elsewhere. There was a little-known fact that almost every Italian knew somebody who knew somebody who had a castle to sell or a "da Vinci" in their attic. There was no shortage of castles, old art, and Tuscan homes. Every Italian we knew, regardless of their income, had vacation homes in the Alps and beach houses in Sardinia. Even Leopoldo, our dog walker, had a beach house in Puglia. Italians were, as they say, cash poor, property rich. And since Michael was a New York businessman who worked in finance and had a large rolodex of contacts of investors with private equity to invest, he had become inundated with deals from local Italians offering to sell everything from Donatello sculptures to luxury villas in the Tuscan countryside.

One of these Italians was Alberto Borghi, who lived in a castle near Modena with an extensive car collection. He asked Michael if he knew anyone interested in buying a Ferrari 275 GTB for a million and a half. Michael went searching but also contacted someone from the department of Ferrari Classics to inspect the car for sale. The Ferrari Classics department restores and certifies classic automobiles and has them all cataloged, with production information on every Ferrari that had ever left the factory, racing cars and road models. The inspector brought his logs to Alberto's castle, and after checking the records, he determined that the Ferrari 275 GTB was what the old man claimed. After that, Michael found a Swiss buyer, and Alberto gave Michael the certificate of ownership and documents. We were expecting the sale to close soon.

Yet, the most interesting deal so far was the sale of the Palermitana Soccer team.

Beppe and Michael had gone to see il Commendatore, the owner of the Palermitana Soccer Club. They drove to il Commendatore's luxurious villa in a town in the northeastern region of Italy, near Venice, not far from the Adriatic Sea. They ate lunch on the usual Italian fare of pasta and meats and drank wines from the host's extensive wine cellar. Surrounded by frescoes and expensive art, Beppe explained to il Commendatore that Michael had connections to American investors who might be interested in buying the Palermitana soccer team. The owner offered the team at an exorbitant price, but knowing it could be negotiated at a much lower price, Michael signed the required nondisclosure agreements and requested team documents. He needed to see their financials.

"Documents?" il Commendatore asked, as if Michael was asking Donald Trump for his tax returns. This turned into heave-ho, and time went by, and il Commendatore was not forthcoming. This was vexing. It felt like the owner was hiding something. Weeks went by, and Michael still had not received the documents, so he dropped the whole thing.

Then the owner's financial shenanigans came to light in the press. It was discovered that he had been cooking the books with the team's money, and he was put under house arrest. In his "absence," he made Valentina—the woman we met in Palermo with Beppe and Antonella—a controlling shareholder and the custodian of the team, even though everyone knew that il Commendatore was still calling the shots from the shadows. Around this time, Valentina made a call to Michael and assured him that "we are serious about selling the team." Loosely translated: il Commendatore was afraid of going to prison and wanted to unload the team as quickly as possible.

"Call your friends at Jersey Capital," I said to Michael. Jersey Capital was an American ten-billion-dollar investment firm that Michael had consulted for in the past.

"I did," Michael said, "and they said they aren't interested."

"Then call your other contacts," I said, anxious for us to make money and do something that would help Beppe. "There's got to be someone who wants to buy the team."

"I already called half a dozen hedge funds," Michael said, "and when I utter the word 'Sicily,' they laugh."

It was bad enough that Italy was consistently regarded as the most corrupt country in the Eurozone. Everyone knew that the South of Italy, Sicily in particular, was full of corruption and mob-influenced. Still, Michael continued to be hopeful that Jersey Capital would at least look at the deal. He knew well enough that hedge funds sometimes do not have the bandwidth to listen to certain deals at certain times. Timing was half the trick.

Michael restructured the deal and presented it several times to Jersey Capital until, finally, it started to look attractive. There was no denying that buying the team looked good on paper. It had the potential to make many millions, especially if the team went back to Serie A.

In the meantime, Michael and Valentina were becoming fast friends, and they spoke on the phone often. She begged Michael to "save" the team by finding someone to invest in them. He told her that it wasn't an easy task, but he'd do the best he could. Valentina was feeling pressure to unload the team while also trying to keep her jailed boss from losing everything.

And then, like a bright lightning bolt from the sky, Jersey Capital put in a bid. We rubbed our eyes to make sure we weren't in a dream, as the hedge fund stated that they would give the team 2.5 million euros for an option to buy if they made it back into Serie A for the following season, which meant they would acquire the club at a bargain rate but also assume its massive debt position. This was a godsend for the club, Michael told me, and it was enthusiastically received.

Michael contacted the Italian director at Jersey Capital. Rocco was a fast-talking young gun who graduated from Milan's prestigious business school, Bocconi. In his early thirties, he was voted by *Forbes* as one of the top hedge fund managers in Italy. Being an Italian male, Rocco was naturally interested in soccer. He said he'd work on the deal with Michael.

The Italian press got wind that an American hedge fund was going to buy the football team, and this resulted in Rocco getting bombarded with calls from reporters. The sports pages from all over Italy were writing columns about the most fortunate turn of events for the Sicilian team. The popular paper, *Gazzetta dello Sport*, which sold daily at every kiosk in the country and was read by all Italians, wrote about it. This paper was like the Bible for sports in Italy, but especially soccer. The paper referred to Michael as an emissary for Jersey Capital, and they made it sound like Michael had gone to il Commendatore under Jersey Capital's instructions, when, in fact, he met with il Commendatore before contacting Jersey Capital. The press didn't know that Michael had to practically get on his knees and beg the hedge fund to consider the deal and that other funds had slammed the door in his face.

But that was all water under the bridge now. Italian football was dominating our life. I had never been interested in soccer before, and suddenly we were zealously keeping track of the teams' results. My nerves could barely take it, especially when Michael told me that in the lower leagues, games can be made to swing one way or another, with less than kosher means. I found this bit of news distressing because that meant "wins" could be random. We crossed our fingers in the hopes that the referees were on Palermitana's side. The team played well and were winning. Michael and I jumped and hollered and danced around the room whenever they scored, swept up in soccer mania. The team was going to do it, we said to each other. They were going to fight their way to the top!

In the meantime, the lawyers from both sides of the deal were negotiating and exchanging documents in preparation of the contract. Everyone was on edge. The Palermo newspapers were describing the negotiations as intense. "Palermitana is about to move to a fund that is finally known and has significant economic resources," *Giornale di Sicilia* wrote. "The deal should close by the end of April."

Then, out of the blue, in the middle of all this excitement and hope, Valentina informed Michael that there was another interested party. Someone else wanted to buy the team. "Like I hadn't heard that line before," Michael said to me with heavy sarcasm. He was suspicious that this other buyer happened to appear on the scene just when Valentina and Jersey Capital began negotiating.

However, it was not a ruse. Another group had thrown their hat into the ring. They were two brothers with questionable backgrounds.

"Who are these guys anyway?" I asked Michael.

"They own a travel agency in Rome," he said, letting out a long, dejected sigh.

"Jersey Capital is competing with travel agents?"

"Yup." Then gave a hint that the travel agency might be a cover-up for the brothers' nefarious activities.

"Then clearly this is a no-brainer," I said. "Obviously Valentina will sign with Jersey Capital!"

"You'd think so, wouldn't you?" His tone left me uneasy and confused.

As the contract was being discussed, my friend Karla was visiting. In Rome, Karla and I were on a Vespa tour. We were each partnered with a sexy Italian Vespa driver. My driver was Fabrizio, and Karla's was Alessandro. Michael kept calling to give me blow-by-blows on the deal. One minute he thought the deal was going through, but then, while speeding through Rome's traffic, the cool breeze in our faces, holding the waists of our prospective drivers, Michael called again. I told Fabrizio to pull over. Karla and Alessandro waited nearby, Vespa motor idling. Michael told me he didn't think the deal was going to happen.

"It's been fucking insane," he said. "During our last meeting, the lawyers representing the team said, on a recorded line, that they want Jersey Capital to cover up the fact that the team's owner and managers have committed fraud! No one could believe their ears!"

"Are you serious?" I said, roaring traffic sounds vibrating around me.

"Yeah."

"That's crazy."

"You think? I mean, how stupid do you have to be to ask a regulated financial organization to cover up a crime, and on a recorded line and with like five lawyers present?"

I heard him yell obscenities, and then he hung up.

The contract between Jersey Capital and Valentina continued to be negotiated with the understanding that Jersey Capital was *not*, in no uncertain terms, going to cover up crimes of the previous owner. If il Commendatore had done any funny business, that was his problem. We thought for half a minute that there was a chance it would go through. Yet, in Venice with Karla, while on a boat tour through the canals, Michael called to tell me the Palermitana deal was not looking good. Valentina and the team's lawyers had sent the contract back with a clause stating that the seller had the power to dictate to Jersey Capital, with explicit instructions, how they would hide the fictitious debt and receivables. Unfortunately, they were still dedicated to covering up il Commendatore's shenanigans. Jersey Capital refused to sign the contract, Valentina and her lawyers refused to remove the clause, and the contract became null and void.

Later, Valentina told Michael that she had signed the contract with the travel agents and that they agreed to her terms.

"Okay then," Michael said coolly.

We were flabbergasted at her brazen disregard for the team, for the city of Palermo that she proclaimed to love. And her decision from a business standpoint made no sense. It was even more frustrating and mind-boggling that the newspapers barely questioned it. It was bonkers. How in the hell did the corrupt, power-grabbing, money-pocket-stuffing side win again? We wanted to throw our hands in the air and say, "If that's how Italy wants to operate . . ."

When we pieced it all together, we realized there had been behind-the-scenes happenings that we weren't aware of, and Michael and Jersey

Capital had been sucked into a theatrical production that has been playing on stage in the Italian soccer world for years. We suspected that il Commendatore and Valentina were looking for fall guys, and the travel agents ultimately took the bait. They couldn't resist the idea that if Palermitana went to Serie A, it would be like winning the lottery.

Everyone in the Sicilian soccer world knew what was going on: the league, the media, the players, the fans, everyone. They knew that il Commendatore was corrupt, but the league power players had stepped back to see what would happen with Jersey Capital. We speculated that if the American hedge fund had purchased the team, the league power players would let them clean up the mess. Let the past improprieties slide. But then, the travel agents had to stick their noses in it, and Valentina and il Commendatore couldn't take a chance that they wouldn't remain in control. Everyone gambled.

In Palermo, a few days after the team's new owners were announced, the new owners alighted from a limousine with a majestic air, wearing sunglasses, surrounded by bodyguards. They swaggered in front of the press, who threw them softball questions, as the brothers bragged about how they had outbid Jersey Capital, the big hedge fund from America.

In a separate press conference, Valentina smiled into the cameras amid questions about the team's fate. But none of the reporters asked her why she signed with the brothers rather than a wealthy hedge fund. Surrounded by microphones, Valentina spoke as if she hadn't destroyed the dreams of thousands of Sicilian soccer fans, the soccer players, and even all those connected to Italian soccer in general. Someone asked her to comment about the sale of the team. "Palermitana has turned a page," Valentina said before getting in the back of a black car, and whisked away.

Predictably, the Palermitana team began losing games. I imagined their morale had been crushed. It no longer mattered to us personally if the team won or not, but we felt bad for them.

By July 2019, it had sunken in with the city of Palermo, and its soccer fans, that these new team owners were crooks, just like most of the previous owners, and the team had not "turned the page." Because of financial irregularities, the team was penalized and dropped to Serie D. A short time later, the travel agents cleaned out the team's coffers and skipped town. They were eventually arrested on charges of fraudulent bankruptcy, illegally paying taxes with nonexistent credits, money laundering, fraud, and obstructing the club's oversight body.

Appearing in the back pages of one Sicilian newspaper, a journalist accused Valentina of shedding crocodile tears for the fiasco she helped create. Italians say, "*Non paga nessuno*"—no one in Italy is punished for anything. We doubted that justice would ever be served here either, that Valentina would face any serious consequences. Il Commendatore was later "sanctioned" from being involved in or being an owner of a football team for five years. *Whoop-de-do*. The football leagues were a prosperous playground for the rich, a place where you could swindle and steal and get away with it. If there was ever a fall guy, it was never anyone significantly responsible.

Not long after the travel agents were arrested, Michael approached me, holding his phone. "Beppe sent me a video from the Palermitana soccer stadium," he said.

We sat down and watched it while Michael explained what was happening. The team was having a practice session, and the stadium was full of soccer fans watching for fun. Then a group of fans stood up and, with their hands chopping the air, began chanting something in unison. We turned up the volume.

"*Valentina! Valentina! Va-fan-culo!*" It was a typical hooligan football chant that was normally directed toward the opposing team, but in this case, they were directing their wrath toward her. I felt my face get hot, realizing that Michael and Beppe had essentially ignited the flame. "*Valentina! Valentina! Va-fan-culo!*"

"Valentina, go fuck yourself!" That's what the fans were shouting, adapting the typical soccer game chant. Il Commendatore had been pulling the strings, and everyone knew it. Not that I felt sorry for Valentina, but she got singled out when there was an entire lineup of those responsible.

I guessed that the fans had already lost their faith in the owners, in those who governed Sicily, the judges, and the soccer league, but by telling Valentina off, they were able to direct their anger elsewhere. They needed to let out some steam and tell themselves that there had been a spark of hope that things could change. But at the time, there had been no indication that anything about this fiasco was going to change.

COLLAPSE

Chapter Nine

"So, what happens now?" I asked Michael. We were sitting at the kitchen table amid the copious ruins of our life in Italy—and not just that, but our life in general.

"I've got other deals in the works," he said. "Believe me, there's other opportunities." He looked impatient, as if trying to convince himself as much as me.

The soccer fiasco had made me feel weary of doing business in Italy. I felt disenchanted. The dreamy fog of idyllic life in Italy had cleared away for me. I could now easily spot the blemishes, neglect, worn infrastructure, peeling paint, dilapidated buildings, trash, beggars holding "ho fame" signs, and ads for McDonald's and Domino's Pizza. I was out of the infatuation stage. I had moved on to a more cynical outlook on our environment.

We may have been going to Michelin Star restaurants, but Michael said that having a celebrity-chef culture was one of the indicators that a society was in decline. It meant we entered the age of decadence, the last of six stages before an empire falls. We were witnessing the decline of the Western Empire, he said.

The six stages of the life of an empire are as follows: the age of pioneers, the age of conquests, the age of commerce, the age of affluence, the age of intellect, and finally, the age of decadence. In the age of decadence, the empire allows the ruling class to make more money than God, and then everything becomes about serving the wealthy and not the needs of the regular people. At the same time, the ruling class uses their wealth to control politicians so they can amass even more money, which, again, comes at the expense of the common man.

"Look at our society now," Michael said. "Us poor schnooks are salivating as we watch, on television, the wealthy eating Wagyu hamburgers topped with truffles and caviar, while thousands, or millions, of people starve." Statements like that made me fall in love with him all over again, but he was saying this as if he didn't work for the ruling elite.

Still, he had always been someone who cared about the underprivileged. He couldn't understand how we still had towns and cities in the world without potable water. It was inexcusable. In Hoboken, he once brought food and supplies to an elderly woman living on the street. She could only speak Spanish, so he spoke in her language, knowing enough to have a conversation and learn her history. He eventually convinced her to go to a shelter. Another time, he helped a stranger, who was struggling to walk, carry her groceries to her apartment. In Modena, he talked at length with street musicians, bought their CDs, and hired them to play at our dinner parties. He felt it important to give artists support and encouragement.

He had grown up privileged, and maybe he carried guilt about that. However, wealth represented freedom, a chance to live independently from the system and on his terms and to take care of his loved ones. In his perception, money would offer him peace of mind. But having a master's in finance and working on Wall Street had not brought him peace of mind, nor had it prepared him for the craziness of doing deals in Italy. Everything he had done prior was child's play by comparison.

"What's going to happen to us when the system collapses?" I asked Michael.

"There will be some sort of reckoning," he answered, "and it will start over again."

He was right. Empires fall for multiple reasons, but gross economic inequality and overindulgence of the wealthy are in there, and history repeats itself. It happened to the Romans, Ottomans, Portuguese, Spanish, Dutch, and British Empires. Could the cycle be broken?

Our brush with the Italian Mafia and corrupt football league officials had made me gun-shy. We were hearing rumors that the travel agents, Valentina, and her lawyers had been sanctioned. Legal proceedings around them had started. With each new development, Michael said, "I'm not holding my breath!" For me, I was still trying to shake off the bitter resentment I felt from the old-age homes and the Fini Hotel deals falling apart. I went into the hotel a couple of times since it reopened. It looked pretty, but it had not been modernized. The new owners did not reopen the restaurant. There was no spa, bakery, or event room. It was functional but forgettable. It had added little value to the community.

Michael said he had a long pipeline of deals that included Alberto's Ferrari 275 GTB and potentially a famous painting. He got a call from Rocco, the hedge fund dynamo who worked with him on the Palermitana soccer deal, saying he had another potential moneymaker. He had a client who was desperate to sell a valuable painting and needed help finding a buyer. The owner didn't know anything about the valuable art asset class or art world. Michael didn't either, but he was an excellent researcher and had a knack for becoming an expert on things.

"I agreed to meet with Rocco in Milan," Michael said, his optimism commendable.

I gave Michael my support. Without support, relationships grow cold. I told him I believed he could do whatever Rocco needed. He was capable of great things.

Michael shrugged, unable to take a compliment. "There's a saying in Hebrew," he said, "that means don't look to be righteous, look to be smart."

I went to the meeting in Milan with Michael since we had spent the weekend in nearby Lake Como. Instead of traveling back to Modena alone, I decided to tag along to meet Rocco in the spacious lobby of the Mandarin Hotel in an upscale Milanese neighborhood called Brera.

The summer was going well. I had taken a two-week vacation by myself to Polignano a Mare, Puglia, in the heel of Italy's boot, a quaint, gorgeous seaside town on the coast. I stayed at a bed-and-breakfast and woke up to an enormous breakfast that the hotel provided. Then I'd go to one of the local beaches (not the one where all the tourists went but a rougher one where the villagers frequented), rent a beach lounge chair, and spend all day reading, writing, and swimming. In the evening, I'd find a restaurant in the bustling historic center. I talked to virtually no one except one of the skippers on a boat tour I took. The vacation had been a glorious gift to myself.

Another good development was that Julia was now attending the American University in London. I had helped her get settled into her dorm room, and together, we had explored the city. It was the same city my mother and I had vacationed in, 1974, when I was almost five, on our way to live in Lagos, Nigeria. Mom and I stayed at a hotel with a bathroom down the hall that had period piece fixtures (this impressed me at the time, and I still have vivid memories of it). Yet we felt posh when we drank English tea and talked about how much we *loved* London and always would. Now Julia and I were retracing my mother's and my steps, now me with *my* daughter. We went to Hyde Park and walked to Knightsbridge and Buckingham Palace, where we saw the palace guards. We walked around Mayfair, Piccadilly Circus, and Pall Mall and went to Harrods to dreamily admire the expensive merchandise on display.

John moved to the United States. He and his girlfriend broke up. She went back to Germany, and he stayed for a while longer, then decided to head back to more familiar ground. So even though I was ecstatic that Julia was now in Europe, I was disappointed that John was no longer nearby.

The grand lobby of the Mandarin sparkled with glossy marble floors, a long reception desk, tables with elaborate bouquets, bars, and sitting areas. Pretty, professionally dressed young women manned the reception desk and hotel restaurant. Michael and I sank down on one of the sofas and looked around expectantly at each person who entered through the big glass doors.

Long past our appointment time, Rocco breezed into the lobby and shook our hands, omitting pleasantries and niceties. He was not your typical Italian businessman who made a show of using formal and praising language. When we sat down, Rocco leaned in close to us, ready to get to the point. "I've got something that is going to make us rich," he said, smiling. He explained that he had a client who owned a Raphael painting.

He was referring to Raffaello Sanzio, master of the Italian Renaissance, who shared the spotlight with Michelangelo and Leonardo da Vinci. Raphael, as he was known, was born in Urbino in 1483. At seventeen, he was already described as a "master" artist. He was a young hotshot, like Rocco, who peaked early in life. When Raphael was thirty, the Pope commissioned him to paint the famous "School of Athens" in the papal palace, representing art, philosophy, and science and ultimately becoming the symbol of the Renaissance. Raphael died as one of the most influential artists of his day, and his tomb is in the Pantheon in Rome.

Michael and I looked at Rocco like he told us he found a pot of gold and wanted to share it with us. Having possession of a possible genuine article Raphael painting was a big deal.

The painting was a depiction of the marriage between Saint Catherine of Alexandria and Jesus Christ. Catherine was a princess from the fourth century who did not actually marry Jesus, of course, since she lived almost four hundred years after him. Their wedding took place in her dream. Thus, it was a fantasy wedding ceremony where Mary, Jesus's mother, was present, because what's a marriage without the blessing of the mother-in-law?

Many paintings from the Middle Ages depict the mystical marriage between Saint Catherine and Jesus. It was a popular theme. In these depictions, Catherine has long blond hair, a crown, and rich-looking clothes, while Jesus, the groom, is an infant on his mother's lap or a full-grown man. In Raphael's, Jesus was an infant on Mary's lap. Catherine stood next to them.

To state the obvious, Catherine of Alexandria was a devout Christian. Either that, or she was a few sandwiches short of a proverbial picnic. The story goes that she was such a devout Catholic that when Emperor Maxentius tried to force her to give up her faith, she refused. Emperors don't particularly like being told no, so Maxentius ordered her to be bound to a spike wheel and tortured to death. Fortunately for Catherine, or perhaps it was divine intervention, they couldn't torture her on the wheel because it broke. Since, apparently, the emperor's torture room didn't have any more torture wheels in stock, they beheaded her instead. After her death, Catherine was made a saint, a martyr, and a revered virgin. Being all three is what made you popular in those days, and it was exciting stuff to depict in Catholic art back then.

Religious art is heavy energetically and often gruesome. It's not something that would ever go up on my wall. When I was a kid, living in Israel, my grandparents gave me an illustrated children's Bible that endlessly fascinated me. I spent hours poring over the elaborate illustrations, and one, which particularly haunted me, was of the bloody, severed head of John the Baptist on a platter admired by the daughter of Herodias. I had nightmares about it and told my mother I was afraid of John the Baptist, something my mother found amusing and couldn't help but share with all the members of my family.

Rocco explained that the Raphael painting had been in this ownership since the 1980s. The owner bought it from the heirs of an old Milanese upper-crust family that had fallen from grace. Before that, the painting had been kept in private hands for centuries, the earliest reference dating back to an eighteenth-century collection in France. The owner had purchased the painting on the advice of a famous

Italian scholar of the Renaissance named Matteo Rosetta, one of the leading experts on the life and works of Leonardo da Vinci. He was also a professor at the University of California and authored numerous books and articles on Renaissance art.

Yet, there was no conclusive proof that the painting was the genuine article, even though it supposedly had Raphael's signature on it (Renaissance artists didn't typically sign their work). The signature was hidden in the emblems of the painting. At an art exhibition, years before, Matteo Rosetta was interviewed about the Raphael painting, and he said that laboratory investigations had confirmed that the letters of the signature were original and contemporary to the painting. He also claimed that the painting was Raphael's earliest known work. If this was true, the painting would be very valuable. Another clue was that the painter had used cobalt blue. This was rare in Renaissance paintings and expensive to obtain. Only famous painters could afford such a color.

"How much do you think it's worth?" Michael asked Rocco.

"Millions," Rocco said, smiling. "Maybe forty million."

"Forty million?" we choked, thinking of the commission on that.

This was an atrocious amount of money for one painting, but we knew this was possible. The sale of Leonardo da Vinci's *Salvator Mundi* was still fresh in our memories. In 2017, it sold for $450 million at Christie's auction house in New York. It set the record for the most expensive painting ever sold at public auction. The story behind it was a thing of legend.

In 2005, a couple of art dealers bought it at a New Orleans auction house for $1,175. The dealers suspected it was a Leonardo, which is incredible. There are less than twenty known da Vinci paintings in the world. And one just happened to show up at an auction in New Orleans!

In Raphael's case, there were 184 known paintings out there. Still, the painting was a huge find. If all Michael had to do was find a buyer for an outrageously expensive piece of art, well, then, hell yeah! If this was the real deal, how hard could it be?

It turned out that selling a painting was difficult, even one that had been attributed to Raphael by an expert. Michael quickly learned that you couldn't simply show up at Christie's with your Raphael painting and expect them to give you millions of dollars. There was a process. First, contact someone important in the art world who will refer you to a higher-up at Christie's or Sotheby's. (Italy is not the only place with a *clientelismo* culture.) Next, prove that the piece is real or has a reasonable chance that it's genuine. Christie's and Sotheby's may still find the painting unworthy based on ownership of the art and notoriety to the outside world.

It wasn't enough just to be a Raphael, Michael discovered. These paintings needed to go on tour, so to speak, gain popularity, and become known. You need to show that they've been in museums and art exhibitions and published in books. In other words, because it's hard to prove the authenticity of an old master, the big auction houses had the power to bless the painting, or not, according to their own whims and biases.

In the case of the *Salvator Mundi*, it required extensive restoration, which left only 20 percent of the original painting. Then, for fifteen years, they marketed the crap out of it until it finally ended up in the National Gallery of London. There, it was displayed as a bona fide da Vinci, and that sealed it. It was ultimately sold to the crown Prince Mohammed bin Salman Al Saud, the man likely responsible for the murder of journalist Jamal Khashoggi, proving that these pieces can get into the hands of anybody who can afford it. The painting, which means "Savior of the World," became a symbol of money and power.

I wondered what was real. Like Albert Einstein said, "Reality is merely an illusion, albeit a very persistent one." I asked myself, *Do any of us know what's really going on?*

Looking at our circumstances, we were living in a beautiful, large apartment, hosting dinner parties, and eating out at fine restaurants. We were still hobnobbing with Lara, Massimo Bottura's wife. She and Massimo had opened an elegant bed-and-breakfast, Casa Maria Luigia, on a country estate in Modena. It was an eighteenth-century mansion with ornate vaulted ceilings. On several occasions, Lara invited us to wander the manicured gardens, sit by the pool or grotto pond, or view their fabulous collection of modern art, including an enormous Ai Weiwei triptych.

However, we had reached the point where our lives were hanging in the balance over Michael closing a deal. We had gotten caught up in our *own* illusion, gambling on statistics. If we threw enough things against the wall, something had to stick.

Despite our setbacks and financial worries, we were conveniently following the Italian way, *Bella Figura*, showing our best. We told ourselves that soon we'd make enough money from one of these deals, and then we'd be able to breathe and catch up. Then everything would fall into place. That was our plan, and we had no choice but to stick with it.

Chapter Ten

The Raphael was in a bank vault in Switzerland. It had been there for years, in hiding. It had been shown in minor museums, and in 2010, it was officially unveiled at an exhibition in Gothenburg, Sweden. Other than that, the painting hadn't emerged into society. Michael had his work cut out for him; he was a long way from getting the Raphael exhibited in the National Gallery of London. But since he was resourceful, he managed to talk to the head of the Old Masters Department at Christie's, who agreed to speak to his hoity-toity bunch of scholars. It was imperative that Michael presented a good case that the painting was, indeed, a Raphael.

Forgeries are common. I read that 80 percent of all art thefts in Europe take place in Italy. It wasn't enough that Matteo Rosetta, the leading da Vinci expert, thought the Raphael painting was authentic. Italian scholars of old masters were given very little credibility. They were considered the least credible in the art world, even though most of the old master artists were Italian! Besides, by the time the painting's owner had come to Rocco, Matteo Rosetta had died.

Even so, if there was a chance that the Raphael painting was even touched by Raphael, it would be valuable. With *Salvator Mundi*, most experts didn't think it was a Leonardo but rather produced in his workshop by his assistants. They thought that the most Leonardo might have done was add some finishing touches. Others claimed it was done by Leonardo's third-rate imitator, Bernardino Luini. In fact, Matteo Rosetta did not think it was genuine. Interestingly, Christie's kept him off the panel of experts assigned to determine whether the painting was authentic.

Michael needed to get the painting appraised, and to do that, it had to be analyzed by a specialized forensic lab. He went through his art contacts and found a contact in the Art and Antiquities Department at the Vatican. They got the painting into a premier forensic lab in Switzerland, where it was fast-tracked for a noninvasive examination.

Then, it was a whole other process to deliver the painting from a bank vault in Switzerland to the lab, and the owner had to be convinced that this process needed to be done if he wanted to find a serious buyer. After a considerable amount of persuading, the painting was picked up by a specialized truck and safely delivered to the lab.

Michael conveyed to Rocco that since the lab report was going to be scrutinized by Christie's and Sotheby's, it was imperative that the assessment process be as unadulterated as possible, and it could take weeks. Rocco told the painting's owner that it would be harmful if he contacted the lab, which had the Don't Contact Us, We'll Contact You Rule.

Meanwhile, Michael met with Luca, an instrument antiquities dealer pretending to be a collector, who wanted to sell two Stradivarius violins (the market frowns upon dealers selling antique instruments). He bought the violins a decade earlier, and in that time, their value tripled. On their first meeting, Luca drove to Modena, from Genoa, and came bearing gifts.

Stradivarius violins were made by the Italian family Stradivari during the seventeenth and eighteenth centuries. Their most famous maker was Antonio Stradivari. He was regarded as the greatest violin maker of all time. There was a mythology surrounding his creations. It was said that there was something in the construction, wood, or lacquer that created a superior sound quality. There are only 650 still around today. It is unmatched. Though this has been disputed by some, it still attests to the quality and attention to craftsmanship that Italians are known for.

Luca's violins were cataloged and certified by the foremost certifiers in London (as with paintings, nobody trusted Italian musical instrument scholars regarding Italian instruments) and often lent out to well-known violinists for concerts. He owned guitars, cellos, and harps, some dating back to the 1700s, with a particular fondness for string instruments.

He told Michael that he wanted to sell one of the Stradivarius violins for ten million euros and the other for eight, and Michael would get paid a commission upon the sale. Michael and Luca discussed the game plan for finding a buyer, and Luca seemed pleased with Michael's ideas. Luca drove to Modena twice, and Michael went to Genoa six times. There seemed to be goodwill. Luca and his wife even came to one of our dinner parties.

Finding a buyer for two violins that cost close to $20 million was a tall order (but if Michael, a Jewish guy, could get someone in the Vatican to do him a favor, then all was possible). In a few months' time, Michael offered Luca several solutions. The first deal was by a hedge fund who offered part of the money upfront, with the rest after the instruments had been marketed and put in exhibits. The good thing about private equity firms, Michael explained to Luca, was that they wrote checks quickly. Other lending options could take a long time. There were meetings and trips back and forth, but ultimately Luca said no. His lawyers were skeptical, he told Michael. His wife didn't think it sounded like a good deal either.

The second was a debt solution bank that specialized in lending money against instruments and would give Luca almost the full amount, then sell the instruments later. There were meetings, trips, and long discussions, but Luca said no.

Third, Michael found the head of Christie's Fine Instruments Department, who agreed to sell the violins to a broker for exactly what Luca asked for—eighteen million euros. There were meetings and trips and countless hours on the phone discussing it, and Luca hemmed and hawed. The man at Christie's needed to see these instruments before agreeing to the arrangement. But, no, that week the violins were going to be on the road, Luca said. The following week, he would be out of town. The week after that was something else.

"In Hebrew," Michael said, "there is a saying that goes, I don't know where to bang my head. It means to be out of options."

"We're out of options?" I asked.

"Maybe not," Michael said.

Michael made one last-ditch attempt to sell the violins. He dug deep in his barrel of contacts and spoke with our landlord's brother-in-law, who put him in touch with a Swiss man, Oskar, who purported to have a close friendship with a Habsburg, the Austrian royal family who were abolished in 1919 after the fall of Austria-Hungary. Oskar presented a German woman, Mathilda, a world-renowned violinist and a professor of music at the University of Berlin, and she claimed to have a wealthy benefactor interested in buying the Stradivarius violins.

Luca agreed to meet her, and arrangements were made for her to fly to Milan and play the violins on the Teatro alla Scala stage, one of the most famous opera houses in the world. I decided I would attend. The Italians, German, Americans, and Swiss were to meet in Milan. There were so many nationalities coming together for this; it was like a NATO convention.

Outside Teatro alla Scala in Milan, Michael and I waited for Oskar and Mathilda. She was flying in from Berlin, and Oskar was driving from Switzerland, picking her up at the airport. We agreed to meet at the opera house at one o'clock. Luca had pulled some strings (no pun intended) so that Mathilda would have an hour to play the violins.

The February air was cold, and we were worried about getting sick. We had heard that two Chinese tourists in Rome had tested positive for a strange new virus. A mystery illness had come from Wuhan, China, and was beginning to circulate around the world. It was terrifying to witness. The city was sealed off from the rest of the world, and we watched videos of sick people in Wuhan being welded into their apartment buildings by officials so they wouldn't be able to escape. More videos emerged of vans carrying body bags and crowded hospital wards with health-care workers wearing full hazmat suits. Foreigners in Wuhan were airlifted out of the city, and among those, 200 Americans were flown to an air reserve base in Riverside, California, to go through extensive health screenings. Starbucks, McDonalds, Taco Bell, KFC, and Pizza Hut were closing their stores in parts of China. But we were entrenched in our own problems too.

At 1:30, Michael called Oskar, but he was not answering.

We waited, worried that this day was going to be fruitless. The other projects had gone bust. For some bizarre reason, that we were never able to understand, the owner of the Raphael painting and his lawyer had burst into the forensic lab unannounced during the forensic procedure and had gotten in a fight with the lab technicians. They had disregarded the Don't Contact Us Rule.

The lab wrote a report presenting evidence that carbon dating placed the painting in the correct time period. The examination also revealed several pentimenti in the work, sketches underneath the painting, including mistakes and changes the artist made. This can indicate it's an original. However, the signature was a crypto signature. The lab guessed that a restorer had written in the signature himself. Restorers often do this; they'll hide the painter's name within the painting.

It seemed the painting could be a genuine Raphael or had been touched by Raphael, but because of the shenanigans, the lab blacklisted the painting, and Christies and Sotheby's wouldn't touch it. It was hard to understand, but what we suspected was that in the world of art, and especially with old masters, the big players like to control the market. They want to be the ones who "discovered it," controlling the process and pricing. They like to use their chosen labs and choice "experts" and scholars. The big auction houses, the UK scholars, and the Swiss labs have a tight grip on this private club, and we were not part of it. The painting had to go back to the basement, for an indeterminate amount of time.

And the deal with Alberto Borghi, the vintage car collector, had gone sour too. A Swiss man was interested in buying his Ferrari 275 GTB and wanted to come to Modena to look at it. But now Alberto wanted 2.5 million euros for the car, when the deal had been 1.5. The Swiss man wasn't interested. The car needed restoration and hadn't been moved in years. So that deal crumbled.

Oskar, at last, called Michael. They were on their way. They were late because Mathilda insisted on stopping at her hotel first. At 1:45, we finally saw them walking up the sidewalk. Oskar was a tall, thin man in his late fifties, dressed neatly, his hair parted. Mathilda, forty, had shoulder-length brown hair. A short woman trailed behind Oskar and Mathilda. It was Oskar's wife. We didn't know she was coming, so we scrambled to get her a pass to the theater.

We rushed through the theater doors and marched on stage, where Luca stood with his violins. We took up positions, us on the stage's side and Mathilda in the center. She played one of the violins for five minutes; then the theater employees stopped her. Time was up, and we were told to leave. We filed out the door, embarrassed.

In front of the theater, Michael talked to Mathilda about signing the NDA, and she refused. "You were supposed to be at alla Scala at one," Michael said.

"It doesn't matter," she said. "I must play *both* violins. This is what my benefactor said."

Luca reserved another opera house for the violinist the next morning, but this time in Lugano, Switzerland, an hour and a half away.

Mathilda, Oskar, and his wife were staying at a hotel close to the opera house, and Michael and I were farther away. Before we went to our hotels, we discussed our plans for the following day. Everyone agreed to meet in their hotel lobby at 8:30 and drive up together.

The next morning, Michael called Oskar to make sure they would be ready on time, but Oskar's phone was off. We waited a while; then Michael called again. Same thing. Phone off.

At 8:30, we went to their hotel. Nobody was waiting. Michael called again. No luck.

We anxiously waited at the reception desk. The hotel lobby had suddenly flooded with people, but none of those in the crowd were Oskar and Mathilda. Finally, we asked the receptionist to call their room.

"Yes, of course. What is the guest's name?" she asked. Michael told her, and she called Oskar's room, but there was no answer. He then gave her Mathilda's name, but there was no answer there either. Had they left for Lugano without us? We hoped that was the case. Maybe since they had been late the day before, they wanted to make up for it by being extra early this time.

"Have they checked out?" Michael asked her.

The receptionist checked her computer. "No, they haven't," she said.

Another receptionist came over to us. "How can I help you? Is there a problem?"

"We're looking for someone," Michael said loudly above the din of people talking in the abuzz lobby. "They're staying here. The man is Swiss. He's tall, and he came here with his wife. And there's a German woman."

"Ah yes," the second receptionist said. "The Swiss man and his wife are in the dining room having breakfast. But I haven't seen the German woman."

We stomped into the dining room, pushing past patrons and a waiter, to find Oskar and his wife casually sipping coffee. God only knew where Mathilda was. We stared at Oskar in disbelief, unable to comprehend how this man—a Swiss man, which is ironic, since I was under the impression that the Swiss were impeccably on time—was perfectly fine with being late *again*. We watched him take a bite of his toast and then slowly turn his head to look at us.

"I've been trying to call you all morning," Michael said.

Oskar looked at Michael, confused. He glanced at his phone. "You have? I haven't seen any messages. I would have—"

"Your phone's off!" Michael said. "I left you a bunch of messages. It's after nine, and we haven't gotten on the road yet. We agreed we'd meet at 8:30. And where is Mathilda?"

Oskar looked at Michael and blinked. "Mathilda?" he asked, as if this was the first time he heard her name. "Oh, um . . . I think she's taking a shower. She said she'd be down shortly."

Michael snorted, and Oskar smiled tightly. "Is something the matter?" he asked.

"Well, I don't know, Oskar," Michael said, seething. "I've just been trying to call you for the last two hours to remind you that we need to go and meet Luca at the opera house in Lugano. You know, the man who owns the violins, the whole reason we're in Milan. We were supposed to have left forty-five minutes ago, but apparently, we're interrupting your breakfast, and Mathilda has either decided to be rude to her host, once again, or disappeared!"

A resignation set in. Mathilda playing the violins was an exercise that would amount to absolutely nothing. We had been introduced, once again, to people who didn't give a damn about wasting other people's time.

Oskar and his wife finished their breakfast, and Mathilda finally came downstairs, freshly showered and not frazzled or embarrassed for keeping everyone waiting. We would be late, and there was no doubt that Michael's business relationship with Luca was officially over. Yet, we went through the motions, managed to get everyone going, and drove off to Lugano.

When we arrived, Luca could barely bring himself to be polite, to any of us. The opera house allowed Mathilda to play, even though it was past our appointment time. She got on stage, while the rest of us sat in the mezzanine, far from each other and barely speaking. Mathilda played both violins, impressed with the instruments, but she never signed the NDA.

After we said goodbye to Luca in Lugano, fully expecting we'd never hear from him again, we toured Milan for the day, our tails between our legs. We wanted to forget the last twenty-four hours as we got on subways. We went to museums and ate at restaurants to salvage something out of the trip.

The last eighteen months had been one long string of colossal disappointments, mounting on top of each other like a huge pile of trash nobody bothered to take to the dumpster. It didn't make sense. Fine, so we were in a country known to be difficult to do business in, but we weren't just dealing with Italians. And anyway, we refused to believe that it was *this* bad in Italy. Living in the country was a new experience for me, but Michael knew Italy and the language; he had grown up there. He was also smart, had tenacity and grit. He knew how to make contacts, build business relationships, and negotiate. Sure, he was unconventional, an out-of-the-box thinker. You couldn't label him if you tried, and he preferred being a "free agent," if you will. But these were qualities that successful people had. Clearly, something was off-kilter.

Where had it gone wrong? When we first settled in Italy, we set out to be a part of the community with optimism and energy. We had gotten acquainted with the culture, food, and locals, knew where to go, who to talk to, and how to get things done. Marco was asking Michael for introductions. Other people from Modena asked him to hook them up with so-and-so, for advice on where to go, or how to get certain things done. When we went out with our Italian friends, Michael often arranged things. He never sat back on his laurels, waited for others to take the initiative, or expected others to make decisions. He was the very definition of proactive.

Part of the problem might have been our denial that we were in trouble. There was regret. I had lost time with Julia and my life in Hoboken. But it was okay to fail, right? At least you tried. Risking failure is a virtue. It meant you had stepped out of your comfort zone, allowing yourself to be vulnerable. It would get you a big ole pat on the back and a "good for you for putting yourself out there!" Failure was an opportunity. This was an American philosophy, and we quoted Albert Einstein, "A person who never made a mistake never tried anything new," and Winston Churchill, "Success is going from failure to failure without a loss of enthusiasm."

In the US, we still had a fighting chance. But in Italy, failure was shameful. It looked bad. It was *brutta figura*. In Italy, we had hit rock bottom.

Michael developed a chronic cough and was itchy all over his body. His nose was constantly stuffy, his fingers hurt, and he had headaches. His itchiness turned into a red, bumpy rash all over his body. Then I got a rash.

A dermatologist told us we had a parasite and prescribed us a thick, foul-smelling ointment to spread all over ourselves and leave on for hours. The treatment didn't work, and the rash got worse. Finally, on one of Michael's trips to Israel, a doctor gave him ivermectin pills (having no idea that this medicine, that had been around for many years, was soon to be controversial). When he got back to Italy, we both took the medicine, and the rash disappeared.

We had other ailments too. For me, my stress ended up in my lower back, and nothing helped to alleviate the pain, not even yoga. One morning, I got down on my yoga mat to stretch, and when I tried to get up, I couldn't move. My back muscles cramped into place, and any twitch sent excruciating spasms throughout my body. I called for Michael, and he helped me up and carried me into our bedroom. Once I was on the bed, I grabbed Michael by the shirt and demanded he call my friend Piera, the acupuncturist who knew Chinese medicine.

She arrived immediately, carrying a huge bag with an arsenal of natural remedies: magnesium pills, acupuncture needles, healing tape, and ginger water. I was lying flat on my back while she administered her remedies, and I gratefully took all of them. She gave me a therapeutic massage and talked about the importance of being positive. She got me to focus on breathing, to let the peace in. If I saw love, thought about what brought me joy, I'd see things from a higher perspective. This was a wake-up call to de-stress and exercise more. I needed to practice self-care, she said.

Piera came back daily to make sure I was better. I was grateful that our maid, Raba, a Muslim woman with a grandmotherly vibe, cleaned the house, and Domo enjoyed extra walks from Leopoldo. But my back pain made me feel old.

When my back felt a little better, I met my Australian friend, Abbie, for coffee at our usual spot in town. When she saw me wincing my way to the table and watched as I slowly, ever so carefully, sank down on the chair, she said, "Oh, Jennifer, please see a doctor!" I thought I must have really looked like hell. But I was in no mood to go to another doctor (though I did appreciate Italy's universal health-care system that focused on prevention instead of profit).

There had also been my last humiliating gynecologist appointment, which Marco's wife had recommended. We were told that the doctor spoke English (I was getting tired of dragging my husband to doctor appointments). I should have been speaking Italian with better fluency by then, but I was no way near the level to talk about medical stuff. My motivation to learn Italian had taken a nosedive, and I was hoping to rely on the fact that English was lingua franca, the common language between speakers whose native language is different. I'm not in any way saying that colonization was a good thing, but Great Britain had colonized much of the world, making sure their language was the dominant one. And now I wanted to reap the benefits.

When I went into the examination room, the doctor said, "When did you last have demonstration?" I had read that only 35 percent of Italians spoke English. Italian, though a beautiful language, is only spoken in Italy and the countries they had once colonized, which included Somalia, Libya, Eritrea, and a small section of Ethiopia.

"Demonstration?"

"Yes, demonstration," the doctor said impatiently.

"Oh, you mean menstruation." I got up and opened the door that led to the waiting room where Michael was sitting, waiting, in case this very scenario happened. "Um . . . Michael? Could you come in and translate?" He meandered into the examination room, and he and the doctor had a long discussion while I smiled dumbly, picking up some of the conversation, which had veered into soccer. When it was time to undress, there was no dressing room or gown offered. The doctor did an ultrasound on me, and I went home with a picture of my ovaries.

"I'm better than I was," I insisted to Abbie at the coffee shop, even though she looked at me skeptically. We then quickly dove into our litany of complaints about Modena since we were both feeling disenchanted and trapped as the air, thick with smog-filled clouds that I never thought I'd see again after Beijing, enveloped us. At the table next to us, people were smoking. We were in a bubble of pollution upon pollutant fumes. As we coughed and waved away the smoke, we discussed this SARS-like virus out of China that was attacking the lungs.

"There's been hundreds of deaths," Abbie said, "and thousands of cases. I think it's reaching something like fourteen thousand. Airlines are suspending flights to mainland China. A man in the Philippines died of it." We both took sips of our tea. So much for being positive.

Chapter Eleven

The strange virus out of China hit Italy—the first Western country to get attacked—and Italy declared a state of emergency. As the days passed, we watched as this strange new virus inched closer to Modena. Eleven municipalities in Northern Italy were placed under quarantine, and then, by the beginning of March, the virus had spread to all regions of Italy. The prime minister expanded the quarantine to fourteen other provinces. Then it was announced that our province was in the Red Zone.

We were in lockdown. Our apartment doors weren't being welded shut like in China, but our movement was severely restricted. We could not leave the city unless under special circumstances. There was a curfew. We were not allowed to gather in groups. All events—weddings, funerals—had been canceled. All the schools closed, plus government offices and libraries. All nonessential businesses closed. The authorities said the restrictions would last for two weeks. To us, this seemed like an unimaginatively long time to be stuck at home by orders of the government.

At the end of two weeks, the authorities extended the lockdown. What followed were unclear and ubiquitous rules. We were told that if you went to another city in Italy, you had to quarantine there for fourteen days. Others said the police would stop anyone leaving the city, yet we heard we could leave if we had a good reason. Some said that if we left the city and neglected to report to the police, we could get arrested. Others said that wasn't true.

In the 1970s and '80s, I spent my formative years in Africa and Asia. I had been exposed to a litany of pandemics, from cholera to typhoid, plus I had witnessed coups d'état, despotic governments, and terrorist attacks. You could say that I was kind of used to world events interfering with my life. I was hardwired for adventure. I was ready for it. But when it was announced that we were in the Red Zone, it was like something in a sci-fi movie. It was apocalyptic, like we were contaminated now. Danger puts our senses on high alert. We become vividly aware of our surroundings. You can sense the invisible partition between this life and the next one. It's an eerie promise of deliverance.

Michael and I discussed ways of escaping like we were convicts in a high-security penitentiary, drawing up and mapping out escape routes. We made a list of the places we could go. An apartment was available in London. Michael had several business contacts there. He could maybe get a work permit/permission thing, he said. Then again, London was shutting down. Italy was ahead—if you wanted to call it that—after Asia, in terms of the lockdown, so we certainly didn't want to go backward.

So we stayed. We were afraid that if we managed to escape, we wouldn't be allowed back in. Then we'd find ourselves wandering around the world like refugees. Besides, both Michael and I were fighting colds (or were we infected with the virus?), and we couldn't help but have visions of being in a hospital on a ventilator, surrounded by people in hazmat suits, and cut off from family and friends. I read that Italy couldn't handle the number of patients being brought in, and their staff was overworked. Would other countries face this same problem if they had to deal with the same percentage of cases? We looked at the numbers—comparing Italy to other countries, including China, South Korea, and Iran—and noticed, assuming the numbers were accurate, that in Italy, 6 percent of those infected were dying, compared to less than half that in other countries, and in most cases, not even a full percentage. Was it because Italy's population was disproportionately old? Michael knew from his old-age home project that the cities hardest hit were in Lombardy, where most nursing homes were located. Yet all of Italy was being treated as the same. The southern part of Italy was not seeing the same number of deaths.

It was a time of great anxiety. We nervously wanted to chew our fingernails, but we didn't dare put our hands in our mouths. We didn't even touch our faces. We watched the emotional videos of the Italians singing from their balconies, and we gazed at the Italian flags that were increasingly being displayed and hung on buildings along with signs saying, "Andrá tutto bene." We were proud that in Modena no one was hoarding toilet paper, unlike in the US, where people were starting to panic.

To make ourselves feel better, we talked about the good things that had come out of the crisis. The "silver linings," as my American friend Wayne called them one day on the phone. Together, we listed these silver linings: how people were reconnecting after many years in some cases, how the environment was getting a rest since there were fewer cars on the road and planes in the air, how people were going back to appreciating the simpler ways of life, how many were going back to nature, and how some people were learning new skills, learning to do things they would otherwise hire out, like me when I groomed Domo myself.

In the quiet, I became more aware of my environment. Across the street, the neighbors had a large parrot in an outside cage that wouldn't stop squawking (I sympathized), and in another building, a man sang opera every afternoon with his windows open, which was lovely and brightened my mood. I had never noticed that before.

Throughout the world, we were feeling camaraderie and connection with our communities; we were all stuck on the same sinking boat. Crises bond people together. This is one of the definite upsides to a crisis. For a moment, the world didn't just stop; it was brought together, bonded by the common enemy of the virus—and not each other, for a change. It was a beautiful thing to witness. It made us think well of humanity as each country got hit, and the rest of us, particularly those already going through it, sent love vibes. And since the virus was circling the globe, those who had experienced it first were like the mentors for those preparing for the storm. Even the Chinese were looked upon as the benevolent country, sending experts and doctors to hard-hit Italy. China came to the rescue when Italy's EU brethren shut their borders to them. Despite our worldwide bonding, unified Europe seemed no more.

Then all the goodwill took an ominous turn. At some point in the crisis—I can't pinpoint exactly when—there was an audible snap where the line between conquering a virus and protecting the population twisted into control and political agendas. This, at least, was clear to Michael and me. Maybe we were more sensitive to it since we already didn't trust governments, bureaucracies, or politicians (then again, neither did Italians, I thought). We no longer saw a world helping each other but a world full of people living in fear. A world of judgment, looking for blame, which turned into name-calling and finger pointing. Collectively, we not only sealed our doors but our hearts too. Where once it was celebrated to be rebellious and free, it was now a very bad thing to be. Since Michael and I were the rebellious types, always outsiders, we suddenly felt persona non grata.

All this had turned into the proverbial icing on the cake. Before, I *felt* trapped in Modena; now I was *actually* trapped in Modena. The government clamped down a set of draconian rules that would have felt quite at home during the Fascist Period in Italy. We could not walk any farther than a kilometer from our home. We had to walk alone. No more strolls with the family. The government circulated a form on the internet that changed daily, and when we left the house, we were supposed to carry, on our person, the right forms. The authorities could stop any one of us and ask us for these papers. The parks were eventually closed too. The police and military circled the neighborhoods to make sure no one entered the parks or was walking in groups.

Before COVID-19, the parks around Modena were places where drug dealers and drunks congregated, with no cops in sight, or if the cops were around, they looked on with benign indifference. Now the authorities were on the lookout for the assailant walking next to someone or straying a bit too far from their abode. Suddenly, the police were doing their job, or *a* job, if fining people without their papers while they trekked to the grocery store could be considered police work. Michael and I were incensed and pushed our luck, rebelliously walking together when we took Domo out, the rebels that we were.

We got stopped by the military police twice. Both times, they wanted to see our papers, but we didn't have our papers since we thought having papers to walk around the neighborhood was "too Gestapo." We told the police we were married. It was ridiculous that we couldn't walk together, since, like most married people, we slept in the same bed.

Unfazed by our rant, the police asked for proof that we were married. *You want to see our marriage license too? To go for a walk?* Why were we the only ones who found this ludicrous?

Each country was handling the crisis a little differently. In the US, a portion of the population were defying the mandates, but we didn't see much of that in Italy. Most of my friends and family (in Italy and the US) thought it was imperative to follow the rules and mandates because we were in a crisis, and therefore everyone needed to cooperate. I understood, but it frightened me how quickly we, as a population, were willing to drop our democratic principles. Where was the debate, Michael and I asked? Where was the scrutiny? Why were we getting questioned for questioning? Sacrifice to ease the impact of a virus was one thing, but it was another to restrict every movement of a citizen's life, with no transparency and no accountability from the governing bodies. Where was the line to be drawn, we ask? And anyway, during the lockdown, we didn't see disobedience as a problem in Italy. On the contrary, the Italians were very obedient, yet, more than ever, restricted and controlled.

For us, it was surreal, like we were not in the world we had once known but were now wandering around somewhere unfamiliar. It was strange because we had seen a lot of the world between the two of us, but this new world was something different. It was smaller, more sterile, and being sterile, hygienic, and germ-free was not always a good thing. It also meant it was unimaginative and cold. Michael and I were suddenly foreigners, and I don't mean in a country. It was all foreign. It made me doubt myself, my beliefs, and my instincts. It also put Michael and me in a strange position politically. I had never voted for a Republican in a US election—but we were no longer identifying with the left either anymore. It felt discombobulated and weird, like the world had turned upside down. But one thing was for sure: there was no escaping. To me, this was a frightening revelation.

The unquestioning obedience of Italians was perplexing since we had spent the last two years witnessing a population that was anything but obedient. Italians were known for being a little lawless, bending rules, skirting around the system. *Clientelismo*, remember? The distance between the government and citizenry was vast, which naturally bred individualism and a laissez-faire attitude toward laws. To be *furbo*, or cunning, was admired in Italy; to be *ingenuito*, or gullible, was to be avoided. Luigi Barzini, an Italian writer and politician, wrote *The Italians* and discussed how Italians don't believe anything can be trusted. They never trust anyone outside their family. And yet, Italians, historically the least trusting and compliant of all Western Europe, were now suddenly one of the most unresisting. It happened in an instant. To bring the point home, the Swedes were acting more rebellious! We went from being laissez-faire about rules—except for in food and fashion—to having our every move monitored. And being fine with that.

As the number of lockdown days increased, we became more concerned and paranoid. We dutifully wore our masks, washed our hands incessantly, and wiped down all the surfaces of our house daily, including phones, computers, door handles, light switches, anything that was touched frequently. We were not taking the elevator anymore. We were not socializing. If we happened to see someone on the street that we knew, we'd awkwardly stand at a distance. It was odd since Italians were normally touchy-kissy when they greeted each other. Now barely a wave. Seeing this was a shock to the system.

The Italian authorities gave us the bad news of lockdown durations in increments, always with a hint that they might extend it farther. This was what is colloquially known as "the salami method." How do you cut salami? One small piece at a time. This made us grumpy and cynical. Either the government had no idea what they were doing, or they were deliberately deceiving us. Not only that, but the restrictions got more severe. We were now told we couldn't jog. No exercise was permitted on public property. From our apartment windows, I watched police cars circle the neighborhood, bellowing through a loudspeaker that no one could exercise in the parks.

It became eerily quiet. If you have ever been in Israel during Yom Kippur, where everything stops for twenty-four hours, with no cars or planes operating, then you'll understand how quiet it was. It was even more quiet than when everyone went to the beach in August. Nobody but a few lonely souls in masks would be out, while an empty bus circled our neighborhood. A few times, Domo and I walked to the Fini Hotel. It was closed due to the pandemic. The hotel's reemergence would have to be attempted again under the right circumstances. Or maybe it really did have bad mojo. Or maybe it belonged to another time.

The pandemic had a huge impact on Julia. She was in her first year of college in London and living in the dorms, which wasn't exactly isolating and clean, and I couldn't get to her. Her school was waiting until the very last second to give the go-ahead for their students to leave. And we were waiting to see what Trump would do since he was closing airports and stopping flights.

Then Trump announced he was extending his travel ban to the UK and Ireland, so Julia decided to take matters into her own hands, demanding to go back to the US immediately. I wanted her to come to me—to the Red Zone—but she was set on the States. Like a sick twist of fate, where it was like we were reliving a nightmare from two years before, I bought her a plane ticket to New York. She arrived just in front of the mad exodus of Americans out of Europe, where airports such as O'Hare and JFK looked like frenzied mobs, where if you hadn't caught the virus yet, you surely would now! She was ahead of the wave by a mere twenty-four hours.

Now neither of my children were in the EU—John was in Virginia, and none of us could travel to each other. Michael's kids were in Tel Aviv, and he couldn't see them either. We were monitoring Israel. Benjamin Netanyahu, who was about to go on trial for corruption, was cracking down with his own list of draconian restrictions, including a travel ban, mandatory quarantining, and contact tracing. At the same time, Israel's ultra-Orthodox health minister, a Hasidic bearded rabbinical figure, said that the cure for COVID-19 was the Messiah, and he was hoping the Messiah would arrive before Passover.

In the middle of the night, when everything was extra quiet, I worried about the kids. I wouldn't be able to get to them if they needed me. The ocean between us, once an easy eight-hour flight, was now big and vast and worked as a gigantic barrier between us. In truth, I could fly to the US. I was an American citizen, but there were more questions than answers, much confusion and haziness, and everyone expected you to stay put. Even so, I had nowhere to go. No one in my family would take me in because of the virus, and I'd be coming from Italy after all. John was living in a house full of roommates, and Julia was staying with friends.

I felt despair and emptiness. I longed for the Hoboken apartment and regretfully thought about how we could have all been there. I had largely come to Europe to be near John, and instead, I was unreachable. How had the world changed so fast?

Michael's projects had officially come to a halt. We were forced to face the fact that our time in Italy had turned out to be a tour de force of Michael's professional annihilation. To deal with this blow, he turned to cooking instead of, say, a therapist?

He prepared Italian dishes, such as *cacio pepe,* asparagus risotto, *carciofi alla giudia, pasta e patate, pasta al pomodoro,* French omelets, and smash burgers. We had become obsessed with tacos. We bought corn flour on Amazon (since that was pretty much the only way to buy anything) and watched countless videos and documentaries about Mexican cuisine. For Michael, cooking was a creative distraction, a way to keep his mind occupied so he wouldn't want to jump out the window. It was a guise, but as far as guises went, this one was at least pleasant to be around. It was like having a personal chef—and a guarantee that I'd gain the lockdown fifteen that everyone joked about. We certainly were not going out to dinner anymore. There were no more Michelin Star restaurants or visits with Lara. Osteria Francescana had closed too, and the Bottura family, like everyone else, were in lockdown. Abbie and Andrea moved to Singapore, Enrico and Courtney were in London, and Piera fled to Greece.

One day, we invited the neighbors over for dinner. This was not officially allowed, but we were starved for company, and the neighbors lived directly across the hall, practically in the next room, we reasoned. To our delight, they agreed. Laurent was an affable French man, in his forties, with a very French-looking goatee, who worked for Ferrari Formula 1, and Maria was his pretty, twenty-something, pregnant, Belarusian fiancé.

They quickly became our best friends. The only other souls we saw in a social setting. Every week, we traded off on who would host the dinner. Michael was thrilled that he had someone else to cook for. Even when it wasn't our night to cook, he would proudly carry over, a few steps across the hall, his culinary creations. When we got together, Laurent and I often talked about current events, while Michael and Maria exchanged recipes. Laurent spoke with a soft, patient French accent and would give me gazes of supreme patience as I railed on about the deceptions of the malevolent governments of the world. He didn't buy anything I was saying, not even as Maria's home country, Belarus, had broken out into violent protests over the kidnapping of their newly elected president. Nothing would burst his bubble that the world operated fairly.

Maria was calm and confident as we watched her belly grow, wondering if she'd have to give birth during the lockdown since the authorities kept extending the quarantine. We felt bad for her because no one wanted to enter a hospital during that period, not even to have a baby. Laurent was worried too because as soon as the lockdown was over, it was back on the road for the Formula 1 races. And what if he wasn't there when Maria went into labor? We assured them that we would be on standby. We would take her to the hospital if needed. It was the neighborly thing to do. Besides, what else did we have going on?

Chapter Twelve

In lockdown, the days went by slowly, the sense of being alone intensified, even with having dinner parties with the neighbors. Our household was saturated with anxious energy, and we looked ungroomed and fat. None of us were sleeping well, and we were ragged and moody. The only bit of happy news was that Maria had her baby. Thank God Laurent had been in town for that. A newborn baby joined our dinners each week. We had been in lockdown for so long, we were multiplying.

Most nights, Michael and I sat on our sofa watching miniseries after miniseries—*Star Trek: Picard*, *The Crown*, *The Queen's Gambit*, *Fargo*, *The Marvelous Mrs. Maisel*—and a handful of British World War II drama series (though we never watched *Tiger King*). Or Michael watched reruns of *Seinfeld*. Absorbing the blue lights, we desperately wanted to get lost in other worlds. Be anywhere but *here*. In the mornings, we'd discuss the shows at length, like it mattered. We spent an exorbitant amount of time condemning the world, telling each other that everything was going to hell in a handbasket. Reality was dark and foreboding, and so were we, latching onto the negative since we were miserable.

Sometimes in a release of frustration, Michael would shout something out the window like "*Ci stanno prendendo per il culo!*" They are leading us by our asses! It reminded me of when we were in Hoboken, and people were on the street being extra loud in the middle of the night. Michael would open the window and shout, "SHUT THE FUCK UP!" The drunk, loud people would laugh and shout back, "*YOU* SHUT THE FUCK UP!" In Italy, he never got a response, just cold silence. His words would dissipate in the air.

We also raided the pantry and drank champagne left over from our wedding. We smoked weed a friend gave us as a wedding present. Marijuana was not legal in Italy, but who cared at that point? We dug it out from its hiding place, and I watched as Michael expertly licked the rolling paper, crumpled cannabis on them, and twisted the ends.

As we drank and smoked, we talked about how we missed traveling. Yet even airports had become mini dictatorships that forced people to queue and comply, submit, and be searched. Where once there was respect for the traveler, now travelers were commodities transported from one location to the next. The *way* we traveled now was the opposite of *why* we traveled. We traveled to step out of our environments, to step into other cultures, and come face-to-face with those who were not considered our tribe. Those who travel want to be uncaged and stretch their boundaries. No one was traveling now.

The truth was, we were neither here nor there. We had left but had not yet arrived. It was like we were flying on an airplane, in between destinations, in nowhere land. How many hours of our lives had we been *nowhere*? Now we were on the ground, feeling like we were nowhere. We were in the liminal space between pre-COVID and post-COVID, both personally and on a large worldwide scale. In the liminal wilderness of transformation between a world of uncertainty and inevitable collapse, we were waiting for something to happen.

To help with the depressive feeling of isolation and disconnectedness, I began a group email to my family back when the lockdown had started. I called the email chain "From Inside the Red Zone." It was an attempt to connect and let my loved ones know what was happening in Italy.

When I began writing the group email, the virus hadn't hit the US yet, but my family knew it was coming soon. They were bracing themselves for it like a dangerous storm approaching. They were naturally curious about my experiences, so I wrote about how we were required to self-quarantine, all the stores being closed, and how we couldn't leave our town. I wrote about shopping in Albinelli Market while patriotic music blared loudly from speakers and soldiers told us where to stand. I wrote about how miserable I was that John and Julia were in another part of the world, and it felt surreal that I couldn't simply hop on a plane to get to them. I wrote that I was worried about how fear was causing people to react without thinking of the long-term consequences. And my family members were shocked by the restrictions that Italy was imposing.

But I noticed, as the virus reached the shores of the US and the death count rose, that they—once surprised and shocked over the restrictions in Italy—were hoping for restrictions in their communities. I continued to report on the situation, but I began to hold back from my observations in fear of offending anyone. I also understood that emotions were running high, and some of my friends and family knew people who had died of COVID.

Still, in one email, I wrote about our Moroccan maid, Raba, and how she wasn't coming to clean, not because she was afraid of getting sick but because she was afraid she'd get stopped by the police. Some wrote me back and pointed out that people were paying their maids anyway. Michael and I were happy to pay our maid, and we were, but how many people didn't have that ability or couldn't afford to now because *they* lost their job? Technically, Michael and I couldn't afford to pay for services that we weren't getting. We were taking out loans to stay afloat.

And what about all the homeless people and African immigrants who had stood on street corners and asked for money? What about all those people at the Questrura who had immigrated to Italy and stood in long lines hoping for safety or a better future? Where did they go?

"I wish I could express myself more honestly," I said to Michael one day. I meant to everyone, not just in my family email.

"Why don't you?"

"I don't want to be judged," I said.

"You have the right to your own opinions," he said.

"I know. But I care what people think of me," I said, feeling emotionally weak. I wanted to feel connected but was feeling the opposite. How did that happen?

As the days clicked away, the virus continued to dominate everyone's conversations. Nobody talked about mundane things like the weather anymore, unless there was a Category 5 hurricane or an earthquake. But truthfully, even those things were barely mentioned. The only exception was the US election. Like always, vitriol between the blue team and the red team were flying like bullets through the air. Tribal loyalties were stronger than ever. Both sides were purposely antagonizing each other rather than solving anything. For us, the injustices, betrayals, and contradictory information we were receiving from our politicians and media was glaring. This didn't feel like freedom; it felt like manipulation.

I was raised to think freedom was a right we should all have throughout the world. We were told by our politicians that freedom was the reason we fought in wars and soldiers gave up their lives. I thought of the US diplomatic endeavors people like my parents had pursued. The dangerous places they agreed to live, to now be told that freedom could be taken away overnight.

When we went to bed, I had trouble sleeping. I'd wake up in the early hours of the night when my demons liked to lurk about and torment me. I begged myself to go back to sleep, but I couldn't, and instead, I worried about everything imaginable—our money situation, our health, the kids, the dog, whether anybody liked me anymore—to the point where I was wide awake, and my mind was racing. My thoughts were insisting on being dark. They were telling me that I had made colossal mistakes. Then childhood traumas came to the surface. I told myself that good things would come out of the pandemic, unexpected insights and lessons that would benefit millions of people around the world. But still, I tossed and turned.

Sometimes I'd wake Michael up and tell him I couldn't sleep. "What's the matter?"

"I'm freaking out," I'd say.

"Come here. I'll hold you," he'd say patiently. "Everything will be okay."

And that did make me feel better. Then I'd finally be able to go back to sleep.

When the shops in Italy were allowed to reopen, the Italian shopkeepers timidly cracked open their doors, turned on the lights, and swept up the dust. Amazon had taken over with surmountable proficiency. They sold products cheaper than anyone else and delivered them to our doors the next day. They had everything in stock, no long lines to wait in. I imagined this new Amazon world, convenient and efficient, sweeping away Italy's charm one day, like the shopkeepers sweeping away the dust.

It reminded me of the faded farm towns in Iowa where my grandparents lived—where my family settled over a hundred years ago—the places that had been vibrant centers of community and commerce, since taken over by industrialized farming and big chains. In Iowa, I was shocked by the swiftness of which these small businesses had been swallowed up, leaving the towns looking uninhabited.

This was precisely what Italy hadn't wanted back in 1970s Europe, when the number of small retailers decreased as supermarkets increased. In Italy, the trend went in the opposite direction. The engine of Italy's economy was the local family-run businesses. The percentage of the workforce employed in companies with less than ten employees in Italy was over 23 percent. In the US, it was 3 percent. Yet now, shortly after the shops were allowed to open, they closed again for a holiday: Liberation Day, ironically.

Maybe Italians had changed since the 1970s, and small businesses weren't so important to them anymore. One day, we went to the knife shop to get our kitchen knives sharpened. The knife shop owner told us he would retire soon, and that would be the end of his shop. He said the younger generation wasn't interested in operating a store like his. They wanted to own stores where the products were cheaply made so customers had to rebuy them. Having knives sharpened and fixed was not economically viable anymore—for the knife manufacturers and shop owners. But what about craftsmanship? If any country in the world could claim craftsmanship, it was Italy.

What I also found perplexing was that Italians were typically and historically resistant to change. They were known to vigorously defend the status quo. In the early days of Osteria Francescana, before it became famous, the locals poo-pooed it because Massimo Bottura took traditional Emilian dishes and reinvented them. Italians believed it was sacrilegious to mess with traditional recipes. He half joked how the locals never forgave him for creating the dish called "Tortellini Walking on Broth," which had only six tortellini in total (when traditionally there are supposed to be five in a spoonful). To put it in further perspective, the first Italian fast-food restaurant, Burghy, opened in Milan in 1982. The first McDonald's opened in Rome in 1986.

Now there was takeaway in restaurants (when it was not a thing before), and cafés were serving coffee in paper cups. For someone like me, who had spent my life changing my environment, I rather admired the Italians for keeping a firm grip on their traditions and their strict gastronomic practices and fashion "rules." Italy wouldn't be the same without them or the plethora of small businesses and restaurants that made up so much of the country. I understood the benefits of being adaptable—I had been adapting my entire life—but who exactly was benefiting from all this adapting? Surely, it wasn't the Italians, I concluded.

These new rules had now been introduced and injected into the mainstream. The change would be gradual, but a line had been crossed, and the bar had been brought down. A new "acceptable" had infiltrated into the culture. This was another sort of invasion, I thought.

Though when I ruminated on this, I remembered that when Michael and I first arrived in Modena, we had surprisingly noticed that many of the cafés, where Italians got their morning coffee, were not serving fresh-out-of-the-oven pastries. They were selling baked goods that had been purchased elsewhere and frozen. I had to concede that the history of gastronomy in Italy was not stuck in time; it was ever changing. In the book *Delizia! The Epic History of the Italians and Their Food*, author John Dickie wrote, "Italian food can only reinvent itself by pretending it has stayed the same. Change only comes in the guise of continuity; novelties must be presented as nostalgic relics."

But one thing had not changed. Michael began another project. He abandoned the idea of selling cars, soccer teams, violins, art, and even old-age homes, and he partnered with a man named Maurizio and moved on to logistics centers. What else could be more relevant in our times? Logistic centers were the wave of the future—places to store all the merchandise that everyone wanted, all the material goods that were to be delivered to us by Amazon. This was now Michael's focus, the man who wanted to save small farms and food traditions.

In June the authorities announced that they were going to open the borders and allow us to travel out of town. After three months of lockdown, we were allowed to come out of our abodes, blinking into the sun, and we discovered something shocking: it was empty.

In 2019, ninety-five million tourists had stepped onto Italian soil, more than the population of Italy, and then in 2020, we found ourselves in the unique position of being in Italy during tourist season—without tourists. This was too good to be true, and we rushed to Venice and Florence to witness it for ourselves.

From our point of view, this was a silver lining. However, it was a big blow to the Italian economy. Major cities like Rome, Florence, and Venice, where their entire economies revolved around mass tourism, were heavily hit. "Italy's oil" had run dry. It was strange because Italy had been seeing international visitors since the 1600s, when European aristocrats would come for the art and beaches. Tourism had been a thing in Italy before anywhere else, and now much of the world couldn't get in.

Later, the EU allowed Europeans to freely travel within Europe, but Americans and other nationalities weren't allowed in still, so the tourist spots continued to remain relatively empty. Michael and I were also free to leave Italy to go back to the US, and we could return since we had Italian residency too. I used this newfound freedom to see John and Julia. I flew back to the States for a week. I left Milan, out of a ghostly airport, and I flew in an empty plane, and then I arrived in DC, another ghostly airport, and went through customs in three seconds flat (that was a silver lining). John and Julia stayed with me in my empty hotel, and we toured empty DC.

When I returned to Italy, Michael and I decided to take a road trip. We packed up the car and dropped Domo off with Leopoldo and then set off with the tunes of Grateful Dead and Bob Dylan. Periodically, we stopped at cafés to sip espressos and nibble on *cornetti*.

We first went to Florence, where we walked right up to Michelangelo's statue of David at the Accademia Gallery. Then drove to the Amalfi Coast, where we cruised along the gorgeous coastline with no other cars slowing us down. We drove all the way to Palermo, having to take the ferry that sails between the mainland and the island. We met up with Beppe and Antonella and spent our days walking through outdoor markets and the evenings gorging on seafood. We drove back to the mainland and stopped in Caserta, near Naples, to eat their famous buffalo mozzarella. Then, last, we went to Nice, France, swam in the French Riviera, and sat on the beach with French topless sunbathers, taking in the vibrant blue sky that blended into the sea. The pandemic was still happening, but it seemed far away.

After a week in France, we returned to Modena. Several long months later, we were spending Christmas 2020 with Enrico and Courtney.

Back from London, they came to our place for dinner. Michael made beef wellington, carrots, and mashed potatoes while the weather acted strange all day. First it rained and thundered, then hailed, and finally snowed.

On New Year's Eve, Michael and I sipped champagne with the neighbors to bring in 2021. The evening was somber as we all wished for it to be a better year. There was no hooting and hollering and fireworks this time like previous years in the historic center. But still, I had always liked the change of the new year. It was about resolutions and forgiveness. New Year's Eve signified rebirth, a reincarnation, and the sweet anticipation of what the coming months would bring. Sort of like all the moves I had made. Yet one of the saddest songs was "Auld Lang Syne."

Chapter Thirteen

One day in February, Michael was pacing our apartment, mumbling to himself. He looked at me and said, "I can't believe that prick, Maurizio, ghosted me, the fucker!" Maurizio, the logistics guy, had disappeared. It was the same old story. A recurring nightmare. A sick joke. An Italian businessman tells Michael he'd like to sell. Michael finds a buyer. The businessman suddenly gets all funny and weird and disappears, even though it was the deal of the century. Michael and Maurizio had a meeting with investors, and Maurizio didn't show up. He didn't call. He didn't answer his phone or emails. Michael thought he was dead. But Maurizio wasn't dead. He bailed without any explanation, which made us suspect he was up to something sneaky (or was this an Italian way of saying he didn't want to do the deal anymore?). Whatever it was, whatever happened, he left Michael exposed and at risk of damaging his professional reputation. All the work they did. Gone. Again.

In many respects, Michael expected the deal to go sideways because, well, frankly, how could he not? But the problem was, when you want something bad enough, you shut your ears to the warning bells, even when it's obvious. Desperation averts our senses from things we don't want to acknowledge. Even though I understood this, I felt numb and indifferent about Maurizio disappearing, and I didn't appreciate being subjected to Michael's bad moods when I had nothing to do with it. We fought. We became self-absorbed and distracted, and then we retreated behind our walled fortresses in the form of emotional shutdown. Things may have been opening up in Italy, but Michael and I were closing down. The blackness of his depression filled our apartment, no longer the smell of his cooking or the sound of jazz.

In exasperation, Michael said, "I'm sitting here thinking about how our problems have taken over our entire lives. When was the last time we talked about anything else? We worked so hard for this." We had been running a long marathon, huffing, puffing, and wondering if we'd make it to the finish line, and we hadn't. We were utterly exhausted.

To get away, I went for long walks with Domo, my earbuds in to avoid interacting with anyone or participating in the world. I kept my head down. Now I *wanted* to be separated from everyone else. I took detours to get home to avoid people. If I had to walk through the city center, I walked quickly, and if there were other pedestrians, I impatiently went around them, irked by their lack of urgency—about anything. I drew into myself, shuttered out the world.

I was furious. I couldn't trust anything. The pandemic and all that we had experienced in Italy in three years was revelatory, and it had shifted my worldview. There were no good guys in charge, I concluded. There was no such thing as non-self-serving experts. There was no such thing as freedom, only various degrees of entrapment. The chaos of our lives, I realized, matched the chaos of the world.

I couldn't help but think of the places I had lived in and seen, where freedom was nonexistent. When I visited my mother in Burma, for instance, it was a beautiful and exotic country, but the government reigned supreme. All forms of communication—books, magazines, movies, music—were under strict government censorship. And anyone criticizing the government was subject to arrest. A pro-democracy student-led movement ignited a series of nationwide protests, and thousands marched on Rangoon and throughout the country, demanding freedom. Military troops responded by opening fire on unarmed demonstrators, and many were killed, arrested, or tortured. Since I was connected to Burma at the time, albeit only visiting in the summer and winter, it was eye-opening.

The state we were in was not Italy's problem; it was a global problem. We—meaning everyone on the planet—were in it together, and none of us could separate ourselves from the situation. We were literally all connected, like paper cutouts strung together, an allegory of how it had always been, and the pandemic only highlighted that fact.

While there were plenty of people enjoying the respite from their pre-COVID lives, or just accepting that what needed to be done needed to be done, our sense was that the restrictions and control were a precursor to what could come later. A warning bell, if you will, that most people were ignoring.

In this environment, Michael and I concluded that the only way to save ourselves and our relationship was to leave Italy. Michael's investment projects were unequivocally dead. It was the icing on the cake that the industry that was worst hit by the coronavirus was old-age homes. If that wasn't a sign that we needed to get the hell out of there, I didn't know what was.

It hadn't been an easy decision. The night we made it, we stayed up late having one of those heart-wrenching conversations about our relationship, our bleak situation, and what we should do next. Then we finally reached the conclusion that we needed a break, not just from Italy but from each other. Holding each other in the darkness, we both felt shattered.

We told our landlord that we were not going to renew our lease, and we packed our stuff—many of the things I had been lugging around the world for much of my adult life—and put them in a storage facility in Modena. Beppe's daughter, Talita, the vet, agreed to take Domo to stay on her farm with other dogs, a cat, and horses. We planned to visit our children. I would go to Washington, DC, for two months, and Michael would go to Tel Aviv. What would we do after that? We didn't know. We packed our suitcases for all kinds of weather. It was the end of February 2021. I had never felt so defeated leaving a place.

Before we left, we were required to get a PCR test, or COVID test to fly. We had gone to an ugly medical building, stood in line in the cold, and then had swabs painfully and indignantly shoved up our noses. A somehow fitting departure from our Italian "dream".

We said goodbye to Beppe, Antonella, Marco, Leopoldo, Maria and Laurent, Gianluca, Carlo Alberto, Lara, Wayne, Enrico, and Courtney. There were tearful waves, but becoming residents of Italy was a distant thought. Talita came to our house to get Domo, and we clutched his fur and promised him that he was in good hands. We were putting him in the care of a vet, after all.

On the last day, Michael and I kissed and cried and told each other we'd miss the other terribly, holding onto each other for as long as we could. I flew to DC, and Michael was supposed to fly to Tel Aviv, but Israel closed their border. He didn't have anywhere to go, so Michael stayed in Beppe's apartment in Palermo while he waited for Israel to reopen. He wandered around the dusty coastal streets of Palermo like a lost soul stuck in the void of past and future, of what had been and expectations.

BIG CRUNCH

Chapter Fourteen

I rented a short-term, furnished apartment in Del Rey, Virginia, on the outskirts of DC. I didn't have a car, so I walked everywhere, which was fine because Del Rey had a downtown with shops, restaurants, cafés, and a used bookstore. It had everything I needed, and I was happy to stay put, longing to be in a more stable and predictable place. It was familiar to me. When I was in the fourth grade, I lived in nearby Old Town, Alexandria, shortly after my parents divorced. Like then, I'd sometimes go to the Potomac River in Old Town and walk on the paths in the parks.

I spent my time reading, and I worked on writing my book. I was living alone, but luckily in the DC area, I had a community. John and Julia would come over for dinner, and we watched movies and TV shows. The kids and I often played Sorry, a favorite childhood board game of theirs. The object of the game is to move all your pieces around the board to get "home" or to home base before any other player. I found it funny that we were racing to get "home," putting obstacles in our opponent's way, and laughing about it. Sometimes we danced around the living room to popular rock songs, or we laid on the bed, me in the middle, and talked. When I was with them, I was in my element, even though I missed my husband and wished that he and I, and all the kids, could be together somehow.

I enjoyed the rhythm of alternating between doing things for myself, especially in the early mornings, and seeing my loved ones later in the day. I went out to lunch with my father, or I saw my uncle who lived in the area or a friend I had known since high school and another I had known when our kids were little. My friend, Karla, visited me, and we toured DC. My friend Christine, who I knew in Hoboken, visited, and we talked about our writing. Then my other friend, Justine, who I knew in China but was living in the US now, visited, and we drank too much wine, took selfies, and laughed hysterically, reminding me that being with friends restores the soul. And every day I talked to Michael.

All these connections were vital. American author and longevity researcher Dan Buettner studied the Blue Zones in the world, which are regions in Italy, Japan, Costa Rica, Greece, and California, where people live longer than average. He found that the key to living a long life is not just eating well and exercising but having a community. In fact, it's the number-one most important element if you want to live to be 100. Not only that, but we must have a purpose, a reason to get out of bed in the morning. In Japan, they call this *ikigai*, or in Costa Rica, *plan de vida*.

To further expand my sense of connection, I discovered activists, healers, thinkers, and journalists who helped me understand my observations of what was happening in the world. People who were open to being open, connecting to others and having long discussions about serious topics. One of the people I listened to was Russell Brand, who said, "The most potent tool in maintaining the status quo is our belief that change is impossible." He meant our government systems (though it could apply to our personal lives as well). As a society, we didn't believe we could change anything, so nothing got better.

"Bill Gates wants to eliminate age-old farming traditions," I told Michael one day. This was particularly upsetting since my family from Iowa owned century farms. Michael had finally made it to Tel Aviv after three weeks of wandering around Palermo. "Make everyone dependent on technology," I said. "We might get to a point where the obscenely rich will make it very difficult for anyone to own land and be independent." I might have sounded like a conspiracy theorist to some, but we could already see it happening.

The world was such a crazy, volatile place, but when I meditated, I could escape and find the quiet, love, acceptance, and peace. I practiced being mindful and grateful, and I watched every YouTube video I could about meditation. For me, meditating can be a religious experience.

My first introduction to religion was when my parents and I lived in Israel. We were surrounded by biblical sights. In Christmas cards from relatives, they would ask, "Do you ever go to Bethlehem, the birthplace of our Lord?" We had gone to Bethlehem and seen the Church of Nativity, and our tour guide told us where Mary bore Jesus and then directed us to the Holy Manger Souvenir Shop. Though I had not grown up religious, I had been lots of religions. When I was a baby, I was baptized Lutheran. When I grew up, I converted to Catholicism for my ex-husband, and when I was visiting my mother in Taiwan, I accidentally became a Taoist. I had gone to a Taoist ceremony and found myself the main attraction as Taoist nuns did hand gestures above my head, congratulated me, and gave me pamphlets about what it meant to be a Taoist.

My ex-husband wanted me to go to church when we were married, but I resisted. However, after we separated, I tried past life regression hypnosis, joined a meditation group, and did yoga and Neuromuscular Integrative Action (NIA), a sensory-based movement practice that draws from martial arts, dance, and relaxation techniques. I also did sound therapy, a technology that uses audible sound vibrations to decrease stress, promote relaxation, and improve health. It was headed up by an ordained minister named Roger, who said things like, "None of you in this room are broken or need repair." This was helpful because

I did feel broken after my marriage fell apart. I also signed up for a class called 5Rhythms, where, for three hours, a room full of people danced to bongo drums. I felt alive and powerful.

I attended a spiritual healing group led by an alchemist named Amanda. Her house was decorated entirely in white on the inside: white walls, white furniture, white tables and chairs, and she wore all white clothes for the sessions, but, in her regular life, she wore T-shirts that had sayings on them, like "Darling, Fucking Own It!" She said *fuck* a lot but profound things in the process. The word *fuck* forced you to pay attention.

Her classes consisted of guided meditations, hypnosis, spiritual advice, and writing intentions. It turned out to be a safe place for sharing and gave me the support I needed.

"It's important that you get your anger out about your divorce," Amanda explained one day. I had been taught to internalize anger. In my family, anger was dealt with in contemptuous silences, in some depriving way, or under artificial smiles.

"If you don't get this anger out and allow yourself to express it and release it, it's going to end up hurting you very badly," she said. "Do you hear me? You can't suppress this kind of stuff. You've got to go through the darkness. Get out on the other side of this. Use your anger to empower you," she said. "Don't run from it."

Anger motivated me to get things done. Perhaps I should have been angrier in my life—and less sorry. When I was angry, I noticed, I tended to be more efficient because I allowed my inhibitions to fall. But I had the habit of feeling guilty when I got angry and worried that I would be disliked. I was particularly concerned, at the time, about being judged as an immoral person—or worse, a bad mother. But I asked myself what my mother would have said about it. She would have told me that it was impossible to please everyone, and like Amanda' shirt stated, I needed to own it.

At the same time, I attended a Kundalini yoga class led by a Yemenite named Rani, who wore a white tunic and white cotton pajama pants. He was tall, thin, dark-skinned, had long, curly black hair, and wore gold-hooped earrings in both ears. With a soft voice and pleasant smile, he explained that Kundalini yoga was an ancient tradition that used Sanskrit language to evoke our energy. It combined exercises, mantras, hand positions, breathing, and meditation to teach us to absorb information without becoming overwhelmed. Through deep breathing, or divine breath, it allowed us to become ourselves again. Once, he said, "Kundalini raises our consciousness so we can be higher spiritual beings. It will help you have peace of mind."

When he wasn't teaching yoga, he was a musician. He combined his two passions by incorporating Kundalini chants to music. One day he told me that his girlfriend had broken up with him. It was very painful, but he shrugged as if to say, *That's life*. "Everyone must follow what they think is right for them," he said. "I apply this way of living to everything I do. Even in Kundalini yoga, I don't necessarily follow the rules."

"Rules?" I had asked.

Rani smiled. I liked him and his gentle, openhearted way. "I don't cover my head like we're supposed to when we do Kundalini," he said, "and I don't end the yoga sessions with a prayer. But this doesn't matter. Why do something that doesn't feel right? If you do things with fullness and love, *that's* what matters. Feel it. Do you understand, Sister?"

In his class, I'd listened to the meditative music and the breathing of the others on their yoga mats. Some audibly took in long deep breaths and exhaled. I'd try to do the same. I'd fill my lungs with oxygen and blow it out until there was no breath left inside me, and I'd try to think of nothing. I found it difficult. Thoughts would come in and out of my mind like flashes of light, and I would take deep breaths again while Rani would sound a gong. *Ommmmm*, he'd chant with his hands in the prayer position. The chime of the gong and that one simple word would resonate with me. It would relax my thoughts and bring me back to focus. For brief moments, I'd feel serenity, and my breath would gradually slow down.

One day I told Rani about my difficult divorce. "I am very sorry you are going through hard times," Rani had said. There was no judgment in his eyes, no probing questions. He simply accepted my side of the story. "Whatever happens, it's supposed to happen that way," he said. "We are to celebrate everything, the good and the bad."

After that, there were coincidences and synchronicities that I couldn't explain. Out of the woodwork, people showed up to help and offer resources that profoundly helped me, as if a higher intelligence was pulling the strings while my life unfolded for my benefit. When my divorce was finalized, and I was finally on the other side of it, I entered a new world. I was stronger and happier than I had ever felt.

Now I was going through another dark period, and by dark period, I understood it was relative. There were countless others going through much worse, suffering in ways I couldn't imagine. But for me, at that time, it was challenging. I felt like I had veered off course. Would I wander the earth until I figured it out? Wandering can lead to death and despair, but the punishing road can also lead to a reward. And by looking for the lessons and arriving on the other side, seeing the crack in the ceiling that shines a barely visible light at the end of the tunnel, I hoped to shepherd a transformation.

Then one day, I said to Michael, "We have to have a plan." I meant a plan for our future. Perhaps it would have been prudent to have said those words much earlier, but there we were.

Michael was looking at job prospects. He had applied to things, put out feelers, and was talking to Jersey Capital, the hedge fund that almost bought the Palermitana soccer club. Meanwhile, I was looking too, but we didn't know what was going to happen or where we would end up.

We finally decided to go to Mexico. We had always wanted to eat tortillas made with indigenous heirloom corn. Some might have said there were many things wrong with running off to Mexico at that particular time. For one, we were in the middle of a global pandemic. But also, most notably, we quite literally didn't have a pot to piss in. We were missing all the elements that a sustainable existence required, such as a home, jobs, and our worldly possessions that were in a storage facility in a tertiary city in the north of Italy. But we needed to figure out how we would get off this collision course, and we knew that when you're feeling stuck, the best thing to do is shake things up. To do this, we needed to realign. It wouldn't work to simply hang out in Virginia. We had to direct our attention somewhere new. Going to Mexico would be like a baptism, a chance to wash off the last year: the confusion, bewilderment, depression, bitterness, isolation, and helplessness. Begin anew. We would have to be on a strict budget, carefully allocate for food, hotels, and flights.

We decided to go to Oaxaca, in Southern Mexico, the halfway point between Mexico City and the Guatemalan border. It was the food mecca of Mexico, the most indigenous of all the Mexican states, and what we assumed was the closest to the root of authentic Mexican cuisine.

"The articles I'm reading are saying that Oaxaca is the place to be for culinary travelers," Michael said one night. We liked the sound of "culinary travelers," as we fancied ourselves culinary *expeditionaries*, going off on some kind of odyssey. That sounded better than desperate, broke, and wayfaring.

After more research, we discovered that crops in Mexico, which had been around for thousands of years, were now endangered because of large food corporations. This meant that even most Mexican tortillas were often made from processed corn and not traditional heirloom corn. It wouldn't be easy to find the proper tortilla, but we were up for the challenge. We were proud of ourselves, joining the revolution to save the small Mexican farms still growing heirloom corn. We were going to find the authentic tortilla. This would be our noble quest.

Our upcoming trip to Mexico gave us a feeling of being in control, and, at the same time, we liked that we'd sort of get lost there. Besides our children, Marco, and Beppe, we weren't going to tell anyone where we were going. We also made a pact that we wouldn't advertise our trip on social media either. We wanted to be off the grid as much as humanly possible.

And being that we were in the middle of a pandemic, it was not the time to announce to the world that we had decided to fly all over Mexico because we were essentially homeless. And hey, it's inexpensive in Mexico, and we're hoping our dollar will stretch a little bit farther there. It didn't take much to convince me not to post on social media and to keep that all to myself.

Then, for the first time in my life, I had an impulse to get a tattoo. To mark my journey into another life, to begin again. I thought of getting a circle that signified the cycle of things. As a circle, anything can go backward and forward forever, looping, never ending. I told Michael about my idea, and he was for it. "Get one in Mexico," he said, "and I'll grow a beard." Not quite the same, but it was a cheerful fantasy that we knew we wouldn't follow through with.

I was excited about the prospect of seeing Michael, and I recalled that time we met in Rome shortly after we had fallen in love, when we hadn't seen each other in months. Serendipitously, our planes landed at the same time, though I made it to customs sooner. As I was smooshed in a throng of people, fighting my way to the customs agents, I heard a voice call my name. "Jennifer!" I turned around and saw Michael behind a long crowd of people. "Jennifer!" he shouted again. "Michael!" I shouted back, and I fought my way backward through the crowd as he fought his way forward. When we finally reached each other, we embraced. In the middle of strange bodies, we were alone in our own world. I was in his arms at last, and he held my face, kissed me, and said, "I love you, Jennifer. We did it." We stood there for so long that we hadn't noticed that everyone from our flights had gone through customs, and we were the only two left.

When Michael arrived in Virginia, our reunion wasn't as heartfelt. Having to wander the streets of Palermo for three weeks and then contending with hot, crowded Tel Aviv, he was moody and agitated. He rolled his suitcase into the apartment, wasting no time making space for himself in my closet and flinging his jeans over a chair. In the kitchen, he set up his Moka espresso maker, complained that there wasn't enough milk, and rearranged the pans. He was not as impressed with the place as I was, pointing out its flaws and commenting about the small bed. Worst of all, he couldn't relax, and he was hyperskeptical about my meditation practice and breathing exercises. I felt self-conscious, which made it difficult to relax. I supposed it was because, now that we were together again, all our fears we had been suppressing in the last two months were flooding back. I had been allowed a respite, but now it was time to face the world again, and I was afraid. Michael might have been too.

It was still discombobulating. Michael had always been my lighthouse. When we were apart years ago, after my divorce and the disappointment from my family crept in, I called him crying, feeling alone and miserable. His voice had been comforting and wrapped around me in a protective, warm hold while he calmly said all the right things. "You are a wonderful, loving, talented, giving person, who only wants to live an authentic life that feels right to you," he had said.

"I don't know what that means," I answered dolefully, pleased with his words but feeling sorry for myself. At the time, I only knew that my gut was telling me to follow my heart, but I didn't understand why it had to be so painful. I had found my family's lack of support unnerving, considering that all my life I had been a very accommodating person. When I was a child, my parents said, "Oh, we're moving to the other side of the world! Oh, we're going to live in countries where there's coups d'état and occasional terrorist attacks. Oh, we're getting a divorce! Oh, we're getting remarried!" And did I ever say anything? I didn't fuss. I rarely gave pushback. It was now my turn to say, *I don't want to be so accommodating*.

"It *means*," Michael said patiently, "you want to be happy. Is that such an unreasonable thing to ask for?"

"No."

"Okay then!" he exclaimed, but when I said nothing else, he gushed, "Oh, sweet Jennifer, this is your time. You will find yourself and everything you are looking for!"

Now, years later, Michael was lost. He was wonderful, talented, loving, and giving. He wanted to live an authentic life, but he couldn't find his way there. It was my turn to help him, and I was glad to do it. I loved him deeply, despite our current problems. I wondered if I could show him what I had learned while meditating in Del Rey, even though he was skeptical. Regardless, we needed to refocus, get back on track. We needed to find our mojo and shift our energy.

We discovered it would be much cheaper to fly to Cancun from DC and then Oaxaca. Neither of us minded an itinerary that would take us to a beach resort area for a couple of nights.

We were ready to fly to Mexico.

Chapter Fifteen

The airport in Cancun was a madhouse, which was jarring in those COVID days. As Michael and I dragged our carry-ons behind us and followed the crowd to the terminal, I was surprised at how many tourists there were. We were hoping Cancun would be empty. The airport resembled pre-COVID days. It was like we had traveled back in time. It felt almost . . . normal.

Yet the only way to the exit was through an auditorium-like room packed with passengers, tour guides, and airport employees, or at least they appeared to be airport employees. They had on official-looking badges, and they were particularly concerned about how we were going to get to our hotel. One woman, who had one of those impressive badges pinned to her shirt, led us to a man in uniform behind a counter. Nothing says "official" like a man behind a counter.

"Your driver is here," the official-looking man behind the counter confidently said. He pointed in the general direction of the parking lot. "You pay now."

Michael and I were confused. How did this man know who we were and where we were supposed to go? We hadn't told him anything.

"We preordered a car service," Michael told him. "We already paid." He pulled his phone out of his pocket and showed him the email confirmation with the name of the taxi company and driver we were supposed to take. But the man insisted he had a driver for us and did not care that we had already paid.

As Michael tried to convince him, I stared at the exit that was . . . oh so close. I felt that familiar twang of fear in my stomach, being stuck and looking for an escape hatch. And then I saw him, our driver holding a placard with our names on it. He was a small, sullen-looking man, standing underneath the airport ceiling lights like he had been brought down from the heavens. I pulled on Michael's shirt to let him know, and we skipped over to him and pointed at his sign, telling him it was us! Without a word, the driver began to walk, and we followed him out of the glorious exit and into the balmy night air. We climbed into a van and saw two young American women in their twenties sharing our ride. They had already claimed their spots in the back, like they were the popular kids on a school bus. They barely glanced at us, even as we said hello, and we plopped down like the unpopular kids forced to sit next to the bus driver.

The driver turned on the ignition and backed out of the parking space. He navigated his way around the parking lot on automatic pilot and stared blankly ahead like an automaton. In the meantime, the young women in the back excitedly gabbed about the spa treatments they were going to get and all the excursions they had planned.

"Oh my god! This is going to be *so much* fun!" they exclaimed and giggled about their jungle speed boat tour, including snorkeling over coral reefs and an underwater museum.

"Maybe the tour guide will be *hot*." One of them cracked up.

"Oh, Kimberly, stop! I mean, ohmigod!"

Michael and I stared out the window as the driver shifted the van in gear and rolled onto a main road along the Yucatan coast. Darkness had fallen over the sand, and it looked eerie and desolate as the ocean waves lapped the shore in the distance. It had been a short flight, but it seemed far away from everything we knew. We weren't in Mexico to have fun. This wasn't a vacation. We didn't have any excursions planned.

"I'm getting the sea salt scrub at the hotel spa," one of the young women (Kimberley, was it?) said. "I *so* need a salt scrub!"

"Yeah, I'd like that too, but I'm feeling achy," the other said. "I've been *so* stressed, you wouldn't believe it! I'm going to get a deep tissue massage. I just hope they offer ninety-minute. I find sixty minutes way too short."

"I know, right?" Kimberley said.

Michael looked at me and shrugged. I would have died for a salt scrub and a ninety-minute deep tissue massage. Never mind that the spas in Italy had shut down. I hadn't had a massage in ages. It wasn't in the budget for us anyway.

"I got a text from Beppe," Michael said quietly. I smiled. It was sweet he was checking in on us. "He says Domo is happy."

I pictured Domo running around with Talita's dogs on her farm in the Emilia-Romagna countryside of Northern Italy and then hanging around her cats and horses. I felt guilty that we had to hand him over to someone else. Although, I rationalized that he was happier that way, and his health wouldn't have stood for any more air travel (and where would we have flown him to?). He was lucky to have plenty of space to run with other doggie friends.

Michael began coughing—a chronic cough that had been going on for months, caused by stress, perhaps. The young women in the back stopped talking for a few seconds and then continued their conversation. We were wearing masks, but nobody was allowed to cough or sneeze in anyone's presence in those days.

The van pulled up to a sprawling luxury hotel. Could this be for us? *Oh please, please, let this be for us.* The driver got out of the van and slid the door open, exposing us to the bright lights radiating off the shiny hotel. We squinted as if we had been living in a dark cave.

"Ohmigod, we're here!" the young women shouted as they scrambled over us and out of the van, still giggling, and without so much as a backward glance at us, they disappeared into the glistening hotel lobby with uniformed doormen. Michael and I watched on with longing as our driver pulled the van door shut, enveloping us in darkness again.

We continued up the island strip, along the shore, passing one luxury hotel after another until we entered the top of the island. The atmosphere had suddenly become seedy-looking, with booming bars and Mexican restaurants. The street was teeming with young women in short skirts or tight jeans with skimpy tops, their hair and bodies glossed and long. The men looked like oversexed frat boys, whooping and hollering, heading for the nightclubs with booming techno music. It was a carnival-like atmosphere of mayhem, and this was where our driver came to an abrupt stop, smack in the middle of all that action, in front of the ugliest building on the strip. It was an orange cement structure that resembled a college dormitory.

"This is it?" I gasped.

Michael checked his phone. "This is it," he said regretfully.

The driver slid open the door and motioned for us to get out, and we reluctantly stepped onto the pavement. Our driver handed us our luggage and climbed back into the van, and then, without even a wave goodbye, he screeched away, leaving us standing on the dirty sidewalk.

Inside the hotel, we went up to the reception desk, where we were greeted by a couple of young men dancing around, appearing to be having way too much fun while on the job. When we checked in, they gave us neon-pink wristbands.

"What are these for?" we asked. Could they have come up with anything less sophisticated? Was this an amusement park or a hotel?

"To go to our happy hour!" the guy at the desk said, smiling and pointing to the bar area in the corner of the room. "Free drinks at the bar." The only thing that impressed us about this was that we would be getting something for free. We turned and looked at the bar area. We saw girls in crop tops giggling next to a guy covered in tattoos, drinking a row of shots. We promptly took off the bands.

"No drinks?" the young man said, looking almost hurt.

"No thanks."

"You sure?"

"Yeah, we're sure," we said together. We wanted to tell this young man that we weren't supposed to be in this hotel. We had clearly ended up in the wrong place.

"Well, the thing is"—the frat boy, I mean front desk boy, said—"these bands also serve as a way of letting us know you are hotel guests. You know . . . for security reasons."

I wondered if it was difficult to distinguish the hotel guests from common criminals. Surely the bracelets would keep us safe because no criminal mastermind could duplicate these flimsy paper thingamajigs. Still, we weren't going to wear neon bracelets. Period. Not even if they wrestled us to the ground.

"We'll just keep them in our pockets then," Michael said.

After getting our hotel key, we rolled our suitcases to the elevator, through a strobe light wonderland, and stepped in. "Are you sure this isn't a college dorm?" I asked Michael on our way to our room, gesturing to the blaring, thumping rock music.

After we put our suitcases in our room, we ventured out to find something to eat. We were starving and anxious to try authentic tacos. We found an alleyway in the tourist mecca that was booming techno music. It was next to "Senor Frog," a popular tourist restaurant. We were told the locals ate in an alleyway behind it. Sure enough, not one sunburnt tourist was there. The side street seemed to be the only place that wasn't swarming with people, so it suited us just fine.

There were five vendors with little plastic tables and chairs next to each one. We sat down and ordered three chicken and pork tacos with lime, onions, and cilantro and shared a *Modelo* beer. We spent the equivalent of five dollars for our meal. The irony of going from eating at the world's number-one restaurant, having iconic dishes, to eating street tacos in a Mexican alleyway to save money was not lost on us.

The old us would have come up with a million ideas of how we could duplicate these tacos, only make them with indigenous corn flour, and then fantasize about opening a taco bar in NYC, DC, or somewhere in Europe. But Michael was not making big plans, introducing himself to everyone, or figuring out the lay of the land. Instead, he looked defeated and closed-off.

While we finished our beer in the alleyway, Michael and I were silent. It was hard to wrap our minds around where we were physically, emotionally, mentally, and with everything.

"What if this is it?" Michael said, looking glum and taking the last swig of our beer.

"By 'this is it,' you mean . . . ?"

"I don't know . . ." He trailed off.

I didn't like the way he was looking at me like he seriously thought we should do a Thelma and Louise and drive off a cliff. Was this his plan when he suggested Mexico? Was he entertaining the thought that, if all continued to go badly, we should end it by a double suicide mission? I suddenly felt cold. "Never mind," he said, like he was snapping out of a trance. "Let's go to the beach tomorrow."

The next morning, Michael was surprisingly chipper, even though I knew it was mostly a facade. He was trying to keep up appearances for my sake, and he promised he would stop talking about Maurizio and put it behind him. He had researched the best places to get coffee nearby. He guided me along a sun-scorched sidewalk to a sprawling hotel with its own oasis beach, palm trees, a cabana, white sand, and coffee shop. Before we could enter, we were stopped by a short middle-aged Mexican man in a doorman uniform.

"Are you guests of the hotel?" the man asked us.

"Umm . . . what?" Michael said, squinting like he was having trouble with his eyesight.

"Are you guests of the hotel?" the man repeated a bit louder.

"No," Michael said, his backpack slung over his shoulder. Was it that obvious? We were standing dumbly, just out of reach of the grand lobby, with its marble floors, enormous glass doors, and well-dressed people. I looked at my outfit: shorts and a tank top, with my bathing suit underneath. Michael had on swimming trunks and a black T-shirt with holes.

"Then I'm sorry, sir, you can't come in."

"We just want to go to the coffee shop," Michael said irritably. I knew it was taking everything out of him not to inform this little man that, not long ago, he was practically the private guest of the number-one restaurant in the world, had negotiated with wealthy hedge funds, had consorted with Christie's on multimillion-dollar art, had sat in a 1964 Ferrari 275 GTB, and had held a Stradivarius violin in his hands.

"Sorry, but the shop is only for hotel guests," the man said with a strained smile. Another man in a uniform, much larger, suddenly appeared and gave us a stern look.

Michael glared at the first guy, ignoring the second. "We just want a cup of coffee, okay?"

"I understand, but that's the rule," the doorman said.

"So we can't get a cup of coffee?" Michael said loudly, as if, somehow, not getting coffee in this hotel was threatening the delicate balance of his entire universe.

The man sighed. "No, sir."

"Why not?" Michael asked. I admired his tenacity.

"You have to be a guest of the hotel to go to the coffee shop," the man repeated.

"You have to be a guest of the hotel?" Michael parroted, as if it had life-altering implications.

"Si."

"And the beach too?" Michael said, pushing his luck. "We can't use the beach either?" I remained silent. I didn't want to interrupt Michael to inform him that we hadn't come for their beach. Though, now that I was seeing it, it would have been lovely. I imagined myself stretched out on a lounge chair and being served cocktails next to the aqua-blue, low-rolling waves.

"So let me get this straight," Michael continued, shifting his weight. "We can't use the coffee shop *or* the beach?" My poor husband hadn't quite understood, or he was pretending not to. But it was abundantly clear to me. YOU CANNOT USE THE PRIVATE HOTEL BEACH

OR COFFEE SHOP UNLESS YOU ARE GUESTS OF THE HOTEL!

"That's correct," the doorman said, unfazed.

"Well, that's ridiculous," Michael exclaimed, seething now, his face red. He tended to get grumpy without his morning coffee, but I knew this had very little to do with the coffee and more to do with constantly getting stopped at entrance doors. It was like the world was punishing him for being a little out of sync, a little different. It was saying, *An outsider you shall stay.*

Finally, as if a magician pulling a rabbit out of his hat, the man said, "Unless you buy a day pass."

"How much is the day pass?" Michael asked with his hand on his hip.

"One hundred and fifteen dollars," the man said calmly, with bemusement. "For each pass," he added, as if he knew this would be Michael's next question.

"Dollars?" Michael asked, incredulous. "Sheesh!" It was obvious it was not in pesos. In pesos, it would have been five bucks. I was pretty sure that a beach day pass for an exclusive hotel was not that cheap. Michael scoffed. "Aw, forget it!" he said to the man, giving him a wave, and then stared down the other man as we walked away.

I pointed out that if I had paid top dollar to stay at that hotel, I wouldn't have wanted any old schmuck off the street to be able to come in and use the private beach. The coffee shop, I had a little harder time understanding, but still. It couldn't be a cheap place to get your morning brew anyway, I said, wanting to look at the bright side. I wondered if Michael had thought this through. Spending a fortune on coffee was not something we should have been considering.

Michael stopped walking and gave me a long, measured look before he said, "You go on and on about how Bill Gates is buying up farmland—land he's going to use to control our food production—and yet now, you're acting like the one percent." I stood next to him wearing my nine-dollar H&M shorts, staring into his wild, flushed face. "Which is it, Jennifer?" he continued. "You're talking out of both sides of your mouth!"

I didn't quite get the correlation between hotel private beaches and farmland, and when I said this, he pointed out that beaches—*all* beaches—should be public for everyone to enjoy, not sectioned off, dividing the haves and the have-nots. It reminded me of when we were in the Questura in Modena. Only this time, we were at the bottom of the totem pole.

As we made our way back to our hotel, I did a little research on my phone about beaches in Mexico. There is no such thing as a private beach. In fact, the Mexican Constitution decreed that all beaches were federal property and to be publicly accessible (legal exception is reserved for military use). In other words, people had the right of access to all beaches in Mexico at any time. But we didn't have proof of this when talking to the doorman, and no one, evidently, had read the Mexican Constitution, as all the beaches we encountered seemed sectioned off.

Our hotel didn't have a private beach, we discovered, when we went back to inquire. Instead, it had a pool on the roof, with lounge chairs scattered around and no umbrellas or cover from the blistering sun. Not surprisingly, no one was using it. The receptionist directed us to a tiny strip of sand across the street, where we had to share our minuscule spot with a massive island tour ferry that sputtered gasoline into the water and took up a considerable chunk of our swimming space. At least the beach had lounge chairs with umbrellas. For that, we felt fortunate.

The water was calm and several shades of blue, ranging from light aqua to dark turquoise, framing the white sand. While Michael waited on a lounge chair with our stuff, I made my way to the water's edge, feeling a slight breeze, and then plunged in. I was happy to be swimming in the warm Caribbean water, with the sun shining and palm trees in my view. I swam until I couldn't touch the bottom. However, I didn't get farther than the rocks that acted as a barrier to keep us in our own areas. I looked toward the open sea, feeling the pull of the tide. After a while, I went back on land and settled on my lounge chair. I had a book and snacks. My husband, who couldn't sit still, announced he was going to get us something to eat. I watched him as he headed somberly toward the taco stalls that we had been to the night before.

While I waited for Michael, I watched a middle-aged man in a Speedo take selfies with the blue sea water behind him. He grabbed a beer and video-called someone. It wasn't hard to guess that he was bragging to his friends that he was in Cancun. *Look at me! Beautiful water, a beer in my hand! It can't be better than this!* I smiled. Although, I wondered why we couldn't live in the moment anymore. If we didn't document what we were doing, it was like it never happened. What about enjoying the beautiful scenery for *us*, our own souls, locking it away in our memories instead of on Facebook? I was glad we weren't posting about our trip. It felt good to be somewhere privately.

When Michael got back to the beach, he looked disheveled, like he had trekked a great distance, like he had gone out to hunt to bring home the kill. Instead of meat, he came bearing tacos. I had come to terms with the fact that this was all we would eat while in Mexico.

Michael sat beside me, put the tacos down, took a long swig of water, and mopped his forehead. He glanced around in a daze, as if he wasn't sure where he was.

"You should go for a swim," I said. "It felt great being in the water."

"Maybe later."

"It would cool you off," I persisted.

"Maybe." He handed me a taco. I put my book down and grabbed it. We didn't speak for a while. I saw the man in the Speedo with a group of other beachgoers. They were all drinking beer. I noticed that they had tried to go to the private beach next door, but they were asked to leave, and they were furious and cursing whoever told them to leave.

"After lunch, we should go back to the hotel," Michael said. "We don't have to be here all day."

The beach was beginning to clog up with more people holding up beers to their phones. The sense of peace and wonderment I had felt in the water was quickly losing its effect. I watched from my shaded lounge chair as the mayhem of the day unfolded. We were being joined by many more people. Our little strip of sand was turning into a mob scene of families, drunks, sunbathers, and beachcombers singing out their wares. All were polluting the atmosphere with shouting, talking, splashing, eating, drinking, and laughing. Our hot, sweaty bodies were sharing the same small piece of beach. Then came the ferry again and people on jet skis who thought this paltry pool of water was the perfect place to zoom in. Then the restaurant next to us pumped out loud rock music. Because why not add to the noise? Our little bit of serenity was gone.

As I looked around, I noticed that a virtual wall was separating us tourists from the real Mexico. It was separating the tourists who were either at the top or bottom of the food chain. We were not allowed to invade the exclusive beach next to us, but the rich tourists could invade our beach with their big ass ferry! The ferry engine was roaring, and the people on the boat were having one big party. This was the state of our world, I realized. Humanity was made up of clubs. These clubs did not *see* other clubs. They did not learn from each other or respect each other. Each club had their own flag and theme song, each claiming they were the true visionaries, the ones who cared. But nobody cared about anything outside of their own arbitrary boundaries. Rules only applied to those in *other* clubs. This was isolating and kept everyone separate on purpose. Our instincts to avoid being in clubs were right, even if we couldn't entirely avoid them. Besides, we were learning that things shifted, and these invisible boundaries could change. At any given time, any of us could find ourselves in a different section.

Later, when we got back to our hotel room, we noticed that Michael was severely sunburned. His legs, which had been as white as a baby's bottom, now resembled two cherry-red licorice sticks. He said it felt like his legs were on fire. Yet his kneecaps were still white. Neither one of us could understand how they got spared. "How did I get so burned?" he kept saying. He had stayed under the umbrella, he pointed out, except when he went taco searching.

"I don't know, hon," I said. But I did. It was Mexico in May, and he didn't wear sunblock.

"This is great," he said. "Fucking great!" He sighed and sat back heavily on the bed. "Do me a favor," he said angrily. "Don't let me do this again." I made a mental note to pay better attention to what he was doing. He wasn't in his right state of mind. There was a hopelessness in him that I had never seen before, and it was frightening. His inner Grateful Dead philosopher had left the building and was searching the earth for some other deep soul to latch onto. I was going to have to stay strong for both of us, remain positive, keep afloat. We couldn't both fall apart.

After a trip to the pharmacy for sunburn relief cream, we found a restaurant and ate tacos while enormous birds of prey circled above us like ominous symbols waiting to feast.

"I'm looking forward to going to Oaxaca tomorrow," Michael said. "I can't wait to find the heirloom tortillas."

"It'll be amazing," I said. I glanced up at the birds again. They were still circling above us. I didn't have to think of them in an ominous way, I decided. Birds are symbolic of freedom and peace. Also, abundance and prosperity and good luck. I decided to reframe my stance.

The next day, we flew to Oaxaca on Volaris Airlines, Mexico's budget airline. As we took off, the cabin shuddered and vibrated, and the plane lifted high into the clouds and over the city of Cancun. I had been flying since 1972, almost half a century. And I hated flying. It required trust in the system. I didn't know the pilots, mechanics, or flight crew. Like flying, Michael and I felt we were no longer in charge of our lives, not knowing who had the controls.

After two hours, we approached Oaxaca, and the pilot began our descent. I could see farmland and mountains stretched for miles, and then we came in for the landing. The wheels touched the ground, and the pilot pulled on the brakes until we finally came to a stop.

We had made it to Mexico's culinary promised land.

Michael's legs and face were badly sunburned. He was coughing, sneezing, and had a stuffy nose. He also thought he had a fever and was complaining that his tailbone hurt. He was like a broken-down old car after a long race, sputtering and chugging to the finish line with the fender dragging along the road. But like the true culinary adventurers that we were, we carried on with our "search" for the authentic heirloom taco. Or maybe it was really about our search for answers. A portal. An escape hatch. I didn't know anymore.

To our delight, we found an organic restaurant that served non-GMO heirloom corn tortillas. At the entrance, a woman was making tortillas on a flat stone grill called a comal. Someone explained that they had several varieties of organic, non-GMO corn from small farms in the area. Michael asked if we could visit one of the farms, and he was told it was not a good time to go. The best time to visit was in October and November, during harvest time.

When we ate the tacos, however, they didn't taste as good as we imagined. Fireworks did not go off in our mouths. We felt let down. This did not mean something was wrong with the tortillas or that heirloom corn was not tasty. But our taste buds had not acquired a taste for it, hadn't been refined to taste the subtle nuances of flavors between the authentic and processed corn. We had been eating processed corn tortillas all our lives; even our homemade tortillas were made with processed cornmeal. We weren't used to it. Then again, perhaps we were taco fatigued and too jaded and worn down to really care anymore. But we did still care. We had a lot of work to do if we were going to continue our crusade to save small farms in Mexico, Italy, the US. Everywhere. We weren't going to give up, we vowed.

In the meantime, I was trying to be Zen. I was meditating, doing Wim Hoff breathing exercises, taking vitamins and cold showers. I sat on the bed in our hotel room with my eyes closed and took in deep breaths while Michael was coughing and sneezing and pacing the room.

"I think I have a fever," he said. "Do I feel hot?"

With my eyes still closed, I felt his head. "Um . . . I think you feel normal."

"Are you sure? I think I'm hot, and my tailbone is hurting again." The air conditioner hummed loudly, making the room smell musty.

"Take Tylenol," I said, trying not to get impatient.

I had been so hopeful back in Virginia. I recalled when Julia and I went into a store in Old Town, Alexandria, that sold healing rocks and crystals. We took our time looking at everything, knowing we would buy something. I was drawn to a bracelet made of black lava rock and purchased it. When we got home, I looked up what lava rock represents. It was once a free-flowing liquid that devastated everything in its path yet left a fresh layer to start anew. "Lava rock pushes one to have a breakthrough," I read, "and to ultimately transform your entire life." Everything I read stated that instability and destruction equaled fresh new life. Michael and I were really onto something then!

Despite my efforts, I was a mess too. My clothes were dirty, and my hair desperately needed a salon and a professional color. I didn't have my moisturizers, face soaps, or creams. I hadn't had my nails done in a very long time. I was wearing the same two shorts, three tank tops, and scuffed white Italian sneakers. I was slipping back into my old emotional habits, letting the world and negativity invade my thoughts. The feeling of fear and panic crept back, and the hopeless thoughts returned. We had been stripped of everything, and now we were down to . . . I wasn't sure. We were confronting our deranged mental states, and it was very possible that we had been wrong about things. I wouldn't have bet on that theory.

Yet Oaxaca was an improvement over Cancun, more remote and less touristy. The boutique hotel we were staying at was charming. It served delicious breakfasts. Every morning I'd get out of bed, in a disoriented state, and have a fruit bowl with honey and toasted oats, fried eggs, beans, avocado, tomatoes, a quesadilla with *flor de calabaza* (zucchini blossoms), fresh orange juice, tea, and coffee. It was the best part of my day.

In the afternoons we wandered Oaxaca's downtown center along dirty, dusty streets and stepped over sleeping street dogs. The city had gray, crumbling buildings, and next to them were vendors on the sidewalks selling goods, including seasoned grasshoppers called *chapulines*, piled high in baskets. Greasy-looking cars lumbered by with their windows rolled down and arms sticking out. Alongside them, people were peddling rusty bicycles. The sun burned our skin, and the street noise pierced our ears as we zigzagged in and out of food markets selling *quesillo*, the Oaxaca string cheese, and *tlayudas*, sometimes referred to as "Mexican pizza," plus moles, tamales, and, let's not forget, tacos.

Oaxaca is home to sixteen different ethnic groups, each with their own language, customs, and traditions. It has one of the highest percentages of indigenous people in Mexico. It's underdeveloped and poor, even though Oaxaca offers an abundance of natural resources, a diverse pre-Hispanic culinary tradition, and incredible archaeological ruins.

In the fifteenth century, the Aztecs, who had lived in and around Mexico City, came to Oaxaca and conquered the local tribes. Then about 100 years later, the Spanish conquistador, Hernan Cortes, marched in and began slaughtering everyone, practically wiping out the Aztec empire. The next 300 years were marked by colonial rule until there was a war and Mexico gained independence in 1821. They established a monarchy and went through a handful of emperors in a couple of years until the monarchy was abolished in 1823. Eventually, a man named Porfirio Diaz came along, who ruled for thirty-one years. In 1910 Emiliano Zapata proclaimed that the land belonged to the workers, not to the rich landowners, and thus began the Mexican Revolution.

Oaxaca today is the second-highest producer of grains in Mexico, and even here, it was not easy finding the authentic indigenous heirloom tortilla tacos we were searching for. The non-GMO heirloom corn tortilla restaurant we found seemed to be an anomaly (maybe we hadn't searched well enough?). This product seemed to be disappearing as quickly as age-old traditions. We were discouraged and felt beaten down by the idea that nothing was sacred anymore. Everything came with a price. Everywhere, even Oaxaca, was touched by corporate greed, affecting the lives and diets of ordinary citizens. It was too much for us to fight against, especially since we felt so small.

As we walked around one afternoon in a whirl of dust, Michael planted a hand against the side of a building to steady himself. "I feel dizzy," he said. He shut his eyes like he was trying to shut out the world. Everything was imploding, and despair was washing over both of us. We were getting on each other's nerves, and it was questionable whether our relationship would survive the trip. We had accomplished little on this jaunt, except saving money. We were losing our taste for life and had little interest in anything, even food. We were in Mexico's culinary destination, but the cuisine was not impressing us as much as we had hoped. But if you're feeling hopeless, nothing is going to look—or taste—quite as good.

Michael's mood continued to plummet, and I was trying everything in my power to help pull him up from the dark well he had fallen into. But I was feeling weak myself.

One night, our desperation accumulated into a fit of fury when we went to a restaurant known for its grilled meat and *tlayudas*. Michael ordered slices of beef and pork. When it arrived, he complained to me that it tasted like rubber.

"Don't eat it then," I said. We were sitting across from each other like adversaries, not a loving couple.

He ignored my suggestion and dug into his meal with vengeance, almost in spite. I watched him eat these slabs of meat in a smoke-filled room, while, in the next room, a television blared Spanish cartoons like we were in someone's living room. "That's classy," Michael sneered. The place was dark, probably so we couldn't get too good a look at the food, and the glow from the TV was flickering on the wall.

I had no appetite as I watched Michael eat in misery. The fact that we no longer enjoyed food was a telltale sign: we were in a very grim place in our lives. I reached for my hand sanitizer and wiped my hands before picking at the enormous *tlayuda* I had ordered. After inspecting it, I couldn't bring myself to eat it.

Michael noticed my hesitation and asked, "Why are you being so unadventurous? You're so squeamish."

I glared at him. "You're accusing me of being squeamish?" I said, wanting to stab him with my fork.

"Relax. Sorry," he said, taking another bite of meat. I loathed him in that moment, and I had never felt more far away from him, which was unfortunate since I felt far away from everything else. Our spat took me to a dark place and I imagined telling my family that I was getting divorced, yet again, and them telling me I never should have gotten married to get Italian residency. Even though we hadn't gotten married just for that reason, it sounded so stupid now.

"We are in the poorest part of Mexico, eating in non-ventilated dives in the middle of a global pandemic, and you're calling me squeamish?" I said, feeling my face getting hot. I was so angry that I wanted to stomp out of the restaurant and leave Michael behind forever with his rubberized meat. For some reason, being called "squeamish" was the lowest of the lows for me. It made me feel like an impostor, gutless. I suddenly questioned what we were doing in Mexico, and I began to resent him, as if he had single-handedly put us in this precarious position.

The situation made me think of *The Painted Veil* by Somerset Maugham, set in Hong Kong in the 1920s, when the husband forces his wife to accompany him to the heart of a cholera epidemic. I feared that all this would break us. That we would join the ranks of the others who had suffered through COVID but couldn't keep their marriages intact. The Michael sitting next to me was out of sync with the Michael I had moved to Italy with, the one who had been full of promises and dreams, and I wanted to sob in mourning. Sure, I was an accomplice. I couldn't forget that. I might have once contributed financially to our family, but spending years writing my book wasn't monetarily rewarding.

Now everything had changed. The world had changed. We had changed. Or maybe nothing had changed, and the real world was emerging into the light of day. The cover had been ripped off, and we could see the creepy crawlies, the insects living on dirt and fecal matter.

They were scurrying away to get out of the light, but we had seen them. Knowing this, was it worth fighting for?

Michael stopped eating and placed his hand on mine. "I'm sorry," he said. "You're right. You're absolutely right. I guess . . ." He hesitated. "I feel responsible for this . . . us being here."

"We're both responsible," I said and grabbed his hand, deciding I was not going to let him take all the heat for this. "I'm sorry too. We're under a lot of stress." It *was* worth fighting for, I decided. It was all worth fighting for.

We left the restaurant and walked to the town square. We found an outside bar that had a mariachi band, and we ordered beers. The waiter brought us our drinks and a bowl of seasoned grasshoppers. I threw a grasshopper in my mouth as I watched a shoe shiner across the street vigorously shine a man's shoes. Shoe shiners were everywhere in this poor, dusty town, which left me wondering, *Why would anyone bother to shine their shoes with all the dust and dirt?* Wasn't it sort of a frivolous activity? At the same time, there was something special about it: a determination to keep things clean, traditions alive. It made me feel . . . hopeful.

A couple of days later, we went to the pyramids of Monte Albán, an archaeological site where a Zapotec metropolis had once thrived, starting from 500 BC and lasting thirteen centuries. Located on a high plateau, made up of temples and palaces, it overlooked a wide valley.

We took a thirty-minute taxi drive from our hotel and made conversation with Pablo, our driver. Oaxaca was a dreary-looking city, but as we drove out of town, the landscape opened, and we made our way along a winding mountain road where the scenery looked barren and brown. As we sat in the back seat of the taxi, the windows rolled down and the air blowing in my hair, I felt free, the kind of freedom you feel when nobody knows where you are.

Then, we saw the archaeological site rise out of the valley like an abandoned, mystical city in the sky. "We're coming to the temple," Pablo informed us as we turned up an embankment and sped toward an almost empty parking lot. When the car stopped, Pablo turned his head toward us and said cheerfully, "I'll wait for you." Tourism was down, like everywhere else, and even if he had to wait, we were a sure bet.

We climbed out of the taxi, bought our tickets at a booth, made our way inside, and walked around the grounds. We were surrounded by mammoth structures, and we stood in awe as we stared at what was left of this pre-Columbian civilization. The realization hit deep that civilizations eventually come to an end, and other civilizations emerge in their place. Life goes on. Humans are in a perpetual cycle of creation and destruction.

We continued to stroll along the paths that led us through a peaceful and quiet labyrinth, trying to imagine what life had been like for these once inhabitants. According to the descriptions, life was harsh fighting against invading forces, performing human sacrifices to the gods, and then collapsing primarily from wealth disparity and overexploitation of natural resources. But now it seemed peaceful, and besides a couple of contented-looking stray dogs shading themselves under trees, taking in the breeze, there were only a few other souls wandering about. This gave the place an ethereal feel.

We decided to climb the steep stone steps of one of the main pyramids. Laboriously, we clambered up. As I looked down the flight of stone steps, I got lightheaded and felt my body sway, then took a deep breath and focused my eyes upward.

"We're almost there," Michael said, wheezing.

The further we climbed, the more exhilarating and perilous it felt—until we finally reached the summit. There, feeling like we were on top of the world, we had a panoramic view of the ancient archaeological wonderment. The nearby towns in the valley cascaded over an open plain, and the distant, rugged mountains bounced off the radiance of the sun. Captivated by the sense that we had discovered a secret place, *our* special place, the pastoral view lifted us out of our depression. We were proud of ourselves for being there. We had been talking about visiting Mexico for years, and we made it.

We sat down on the ledge and listened to the silence, except for the monotone hum of cicadas. There was nothing but landscape and stone.

Here, our problems were irrelevant. Here, we were reminded that we were specks of energy moving throughout the universe alongside countless other specks of energy. I was transfixed with this idea as I stared at a city that once had thousands of inhabitants, and now it was gone. And yet, it hadn't disappeared. We were here many years later, sitting on top of a structure that the Zapotec people had built.

"Do you wish we never lived in Italy?" Michael suddenly asked. It felt like he was asking if I regretted that I had chosen to be with him. If that was the question, no, of course not. But Italy?

I was weary, for sure. We had lost our footing, but we had gained a lot too. In the last few years, Italy taught me about food, art, and history. I had been devastated when Julia left, but she spent much-needed quality time with her dad. As a result, her dad and I got along now. We had even, did I dare say, become friends? Julia and John both got to study abroad, live in a foreign city on their own, gain independence, and travel Europe. For Michael and me, living in Italy and dealing with its bureaucracy forced us to look at how systems—not just Italy—worked. The pandemic was revelatory. It challenged us to examine the world more closely. It led us to look deeper at ourselves and compelled us to figure out what we both needed to be happy. Our life had been exhausting but interesting, exacerbating but full of beauty. No, not regretful. In fact, I loved Italy. I loved the beautiful aspects of it and the flaws that were irritating and maddening but also part of its charm. That was the definition of love, wasn't it? Accepting all of it and secretly adoring, or forgiving, the ugly parts.

"I don't regret it," I said. "We were meant to be in Italy, and we are meant to be in Mexico."

Michael gave me a quizzical look. He dismissed our being in Mexico as an accidental bonus. But he became pensive as we stared across the mountain landscape that rolled off to infinity in the simmering summer heat. He mentioned that he used to daydream about us living simply but happily, and I realized that all along, at every juncture, we had wanted to find meaning and purpose. But who doesn't want that?

"Remember when we used to talk about having a vegetable garden?" Michael asked me.

"I remember," I said. That was so long ago. But it was a dream we needed to keep hold of. It was a good dream.

"Our life is complicated," he said, as if it needed to be pointed out. "But maybe that's just us." He then recited a Grateful Dead quote: "Once in a while you can get shown the light in the strangest of places if you look at it right."

"That Jerry Garcia knew what he was talking about." I laughed. We needed to start having more fun. That was the only way we were going to get through this. The only way to get through life, no matter what was happening.

I thought about when my mother had cancer and was having chemotherapy treatments. I would drive her to the hospital. I'd watch the nurses "hook her up" as she sat there and chatted with the staff. I admired her immensely. She was so brave. Her courage came from seeking the very best in situations, from not losing hope that things could get better. At the hospital one day, Mom told the nurses my big news. "Jennifer just found out she's pregnant." She beamed. The nurses congratulated us and gave us each a hug. Despite the circumstances, we felt elated.

On the way home, we sang our favorite songs, and one of them was "Don't Fence Me In" by Rosemary Clooney. As we reached Mom's townhouse in Washington, DC, still singing, we opened the garage door, parked the car, and closed the garage door. Mom fumbled for her keys in her purse and opened the door that led into the yard and then locked that door. She then opened a metal grid, closed it, locked that, and opened the door that led to the backdoor to the kitchen. All the while, we were still singing "Don't Fence Me In." When we finally made it inside and looked back at the numerous doors and gates we had passed through, we realized how fenced in we were—not just from those doors and gates but from her illness—and then burst out laughing until we fell over in tears.

My mother died less than eight months later, the week before John was born. She never got to hold him.

Perhaps my pregnancy gave her the permission to be free, shedding the burden of guilt that I never had a home. We both thought home was unfindable, a blur on the horizon that disappeared when you drew near. It's hard to say whether it was the lifestyle itself or an inheritable trait that caused me to continue to search after she died. The search, like love, wrapped its tight arms around me, suffocating and comforting at the same time. Now I understood something that even my mother hadn't understood. Home was me. I had never left it.

After a while, Michael and I stood up and brushed the dirt off our pants as the desert wind whipped at our ears. We made a steady descent, watching our footing while we hung on to each other for balance.

On firm ground, Michael said, "I don't regret that we fell in love, Jennifer."

"Me either." I smiled. "I love you, and I'm glad we're in this together."

We held hands as we walked to the parking lot and spotted Pablo waiting for us.

"Did you enjoy it?" he asked.

"It's beautiful," we said and took off, bumping along the rutted road. Pablo promised the road would get smoother soon.

Michael got a call shortly after we got back to our hotel room. I could tell by the serious look on his face that it was about something important. "Uh-huh," he said. He was pacing around the room. "I have a business partner, Marco," he said. I looked at him, but he turned his back. It sounded like a project in Italy. *What is it this time? Art? Cars? Cheese? Wine?* "I can get you that," Michael said. "Uh-huh. Yes. I have all that." I caught his eye and mouthed *who is it?* He put his hand up. "Send the documents now? Sure. No problem. I'll email them right away."

When he hung up, he looked different. Days before, he was on the brink of a nervous breakdown, and now he seemed almost . . . happy.

Well, maybe relieved was more accurate.

He sat down on the bed and said, "That was an investor on the phone."

"An investor for what?" I asked.

Michael smirked. "Italian old-age homes," he said.

"What? I thought the coronavirus had devastated the industry?"

"It has, but it has also woken up the market, apparently," he said. This made sense to some degree. "He said he'll pay me a generous retainer plus commissions."

"Up front?" I asked. We had agreed that Michael would not do any free work anymore, not even for hedge funds and wealthy investors. *Especially* not for them. They were the cheapest.

"Yes. The retainer will be paid up front," he promised. He had learned his lesson, and yet he had a gleam in his eyes. "This could be very lucrative." I could see the gears in his brain turning. "The investor is looking to deploy a substantial amount of capital in assisted-living homes and needs an expert in the old-age home industry in Italy."

If Michael had dangled the words "substantial amount of capital" in front of me a few years ago, I would have gotten excited. But I was like . . . eh. I was cynical. Still, this was Michael's area of expertise. He and Marco had spent a decade researching the old-aged homes sector and knew everything about it, more than anyone. It would be a shame to leave that behind.

Michael grabbed his computer. "The investor wants me to send him a list of homes for sale. He wants to act fast, so he requested I send it ASAP." I watched him prepare the file as I plopped down on the bed. He worked quickly and then pushed send. A short time later, he looked perplexed as he pushed the button again, and then again, several more times.

"What the hell?" he said. "It won't send."

He tried again. Still nothing. "It looks like the internet's not working," he said.

We went to the front desk to inquire about the loss of connection, and the woman explained that the entire city was down. "Nobody has internet," she said calmly.

"Nobody?" Michael balked. "No one in this entire town can use the internet?"

"That's right," the woman said. I could tell by her demeanor that this happened all the time. This was life. They rolled with it.

Michael threw up his arms. "Of course, this had to happen now!" he said. He shook his head and let out a long exhale. "Let's go back to our room and wait for the internet to come back on." He turned to the receptionist. "When will that be?"

"Thirty minutes," she said.

Thirty minutes later, the internet was still down. It was down hours later, and Michael was about to lose it. I wondered if I should keep sharp objects out of his reach, but then he calmed down and shrugged, resigned to the idea that he had no control over it.

The internet returned in the wee hours of the night, and Michael sent the documents, though, this time, with less enthusiasm. We both collapsed on the bed and looked at the ceiling.

"So, the investor will get the documents now, and then what?" I asked.

"Then, if he likes what he sees, he'll send me my first retainer."

"Is he expecting you to go back to Italy?" I asked.

"Yes. He wants me to work in Milan," he said. Italy seemed like a faraway and surreal place to me then. When I hesitated, he said, "Let's go back to the States first, see the kids, and then we'll fly to Italy." When I still hesitated to answer, he added, "As soon as we can afford it, we'll buy a house in the US, so we'll always have a home base there, okay? You can come back whenever you want."

"That might work," I said. If Michael and I wanted to live in the US as well as Italy, I had faith we'd find a way to do it.

Michael was being presented with an opportunity. It was a miracle, really. We were at the end of the road, and then someone materialized who wanted to invest in Italian old-age homes, the very thing Michael was an expert on and had gone to Italy for initially. As for me, I found living in the States to be appealing. I was learning to appreciate my country of birth. As international as I thought I was, whenever I was in airports or foreign lands and I'd come across Americans, I'd feel safe and warm knowing I was with people I could relate to; we shared the same culture. So, I was in a club after all.

Michael grabbed my hand. "What's the worst thing that can happen if it doesn't pan out? We hit rock bottom?" He grinned.

"Har. Har," I said, pulling my hand away. I didn't think it was funny.

"Let's look at the bright side of going back to Italy, okay?" Michael said, looking into my eyes. He was more like his old self. The hopeful dreamer I had fallen in love with had returned. I felt myself fighting back tears that my love and husband was next to me again. "For starters, we'll eat amazing food."

"That's true," I said, feeling myself concede.

"We can have tortellini in *brodo* again," he said. We had forgotten about tacos.

"And fresh mozzarella . . ."

"And grilled artichokes."

Italians were not flag waving patriots—not since the Fascist era—but they did have national pride regarding their food and boasted about the fact that their dishes were made from good-quality ingredients and were simple. It struck me that this was true in the North and the South, known rivalries, and that in Italian cuisine, there was little disparity between what the wealthy ate and what the poor ate in terms of health and excellence. The Italian table was a leveling. At the Italian table, there was no great divide. I smiled, so appreciative of this fact.

"We can see Domo," I said. I pictured Domo running around Talita's farm, playing in the Italian countryside, chasing the wind near the Apennine Mountains of Emilia-Romagna. He, out of all of us, had found a home there.

"Talita said he's helping her guard her horses," Michael said, chuckling.

So, Domo was doing something productive. I was happy for him. But what had *we* been doing? Let's see. In the three years since we moved to Italy, we ate at a three-Michelin-star restaurant, learned about Italian cuisine, attempted multimillion-dollar deals, made lifelong friends, tended to the needs of our five children, got married, traveled Europe, obtained Italian residency, and survived a pandemic. We hadn't exactly been slackers.

We then traveled to Mexico in search of answers and turned back around only to end up where we had been in the beginning. Sometimes it's best to go back, turn the car around, and do it again. This time we were going to finish what we started. Complete the cycle. Michael would work on the old-age home project, and I would finish my book.

We suddenly found ourselves at a momentous juncture, the crossing over place, out of the in-between, and into happier times. *We made it. We did it together.*

"Or," Michael said thoughtfully, "we don't have to go to Italy right away. Not initially. I mean, as long as I'm in Europe. We could hang out in Barcelona first. We love Spanish tapas. What do you think?" I smiled. He was still improvising.

Even though we didn't know exactly what would happen then, we felt in our gut that it was going to work out this time. And it did. Michael got hired to invest in old-age homes in Italy and made a substantial amount of capital, finally. We hung out in Barcelona for six months, then rented an apartment in Milan, and got a place in Virginia too, which we made our home base and main residence. However, we never stopped being seekers or wanting to wander the earth.

But back in that hotel room in Oaxaca, I took my husband's hand, not knowing yet what lay ahead, prepared to continue the journey we had set out upon together. We were exactly where we were supposed to be, always were at every juncture. We had trusted our instincts and followed our intuition, never gave up (even though we came close), and kept looking for ways to help the world and invest in our passions. It was our journey, and this was our life. I was grateful for every part of it.

Feeling tears of relief bubble up, I leaned back on Michael and prepared myself to say what I always say when presented with an adventure and new promises for the future, thankful that life was about change, and nothing was permanent. That's what made life worth living. "Yes," I said, crying out of sheer jubilation. "Let's go, babe. Let's move."

Acknowledgments

I am grateful to all the friends we made in Italy and to my friends and family who have helped me along the way. Thank you for being a part of my story. I hope you know how much you all mean to me.

 I would like to thank my book coach, Robert Astle, for his professional advice and support and the entire Koehler Books publishing family. Finally, my eternal gratitude to my husband, Michael, for walking the path with me. Thank you to Ella, Libby, Joni, and my beloved John and Julia.

www.ingramcontent.com/pod-product-compliance
Lightning Source LLC
LaVergne TN
LVHW041944070526
838199LV00051BA/2897